REPUTATIONS

LENIN

Michael Rawcliffe

B.T. BATSFORD LTD, LONDON

Typeset by Tek-Art Ltd, Kent
and printed in Great Britain by
The Bath Press, Bath
for the publishers
B.T. Batsford Ltd
4 Fitzhardinge Street
London W1H 0AH

ISBN 0 7134 5611 6

Acknowledgments

The Author and Publishers would like to thank the
following for permission to reproduce illustrations: BBC
Hulton Picture Library for page 31; The New York
Public Library picture collection for page 56; Novosti
Press Agency for pages 5, 6, 15, 37, 52, 54 and 58; United
Press for the frontispiece and page 12. The maps on
pages 26, 35, 44 and 48 were drawn by Robert Brien.

Frontispiece *Lenin speaking to a crowd in Theatre square,
with the Maly Theatre behind him. Trotsky can be seen on the
right, standing beside the wooden podium.*

Cover Illustrations (clockwise from top left):
Bolshevik poster of Lenin (courtesy New York Public
Library picture collection); *Lenin in 1900* (courtesy
Novosti Press Agency); *Lenin with his wife Krupskaya,
nephew Victor and Vera, a worker's daughter, at Gorky in 1922*
(courtesy BBC Hulton Picture Library); *Portrait of Lenin*
(courtesy Novosti Press Agency); *Lenin Addressing
Vsevobuch troops in Red Square, 25 May 1919* (courtesy
Novosti Press Agency).

Contents

Time Chart

1855-81   Reign of Tsar Alexander II.

1861   Emancipation of the serfs.

1870   Lenin born, as Vladimir Ilyich Ulyanov (22 April).

1879-87   Lenin attends the Simbirsk High School.

1881   Assassination of Alexander II.

1881-94   Reign of Tsar Alexander III. A period of repression begins.

1887   Lenin's brother executed for involvement in a plot to assassinate the tsar. Lenin enters Kazan University to study law. Expelled in December and exiled to Kokushkino.

1889   Lenin moves to Samara.

1891   Lenin passes final law examination.

1894   Death of Alexander III. Accession of Nicholas II – the last tsar. Lenin involves himself in work with revolutionary groups.

1895   Lenin travels abroad in the spring, returning in November. Organizes the League of Struggle for the Emancipation of the Working Class. Arrested and imprisoned in December.

1896   Lenin in prison in St Petersburg.

1897   Lenin released from prison in March and writes *The Development of Capitalism in Russia*. Is joined in exile by Nadezhda Krupskaya, his future wife.

1898   Foundation of the Marxist Russian Social Democratic Party (R.S.D.L.P.) in Minsk. Lenin marries in July.

1900   Lenin's exile ends and he travels abroad. Production of *Iskra* begins in Munich.

1902   Socialist Revolutionary Party (S.R.s) founded. Lenin writes *What is to be Done?*

1903   Second conference of the R.S.D.L.P. in Brussels, then London. The party splits into two groups – the Bolsheviks and the Mensheviks. Lenin moves to Geneva. Having emerged as head of the Bolsheviks Lenin founds *Vyperod* and resigns as editor of *Iskra*.

1904-5   Russo-Japanese War.

1904   Lenin elected member of the Central Committee.

1905   Lenin returns from abroad. The first soviet set up in St Petersburg (August). The tsar issues his manifesto, and the Duma is established (October). The Moscow Uprising (December).

1906-11   Agricultural reforms in Russia.

1907-17   Lenin's second period of exile, spent mainly in Switzerland.

1911   Stolypin assassinated.

1912   Massacre in the Lena goldfields. First publication of *Pravda*.

1914   Outbreak of First World War (August).

1916   The murder of Rasputin (December). Lenin publishes *Imperialism: the Highest Stage of Capitalism*.

1917   Revolution in St Petersburg; Nicholas II abdicates; Prince Lvov becomes Prime Minister (March). Lenin returns to Russia and publishes his 'April Theses'. First All Russian Congress of Soviets (June). Riots in Petrograd; the arrests of Bolshevik leaders (July). Kornilov Revolt suppressed (September). Trotsky elected Chairman of the Petrograd Soviet; Central Committee of Bolsheviks calls for an armed uprising against the Provisional Government; Military Revolutionary Movement founded (October). The Bolshevik Revolution (November). Armistice signed between Russia and Germany (December).

1918-21   Civil War in Russia.

1918   The opening of the Constituent Assembly and its suppression by the Bolsheviks (January). Treaty of Brest-Litovsk between Russia and Germany; the Second Congress of the Bolsheviks, who change name to the Communist Party; Moscow becomes Russia's capital (March). Japanese and British forces land at Vladivostock (April). Georgia, Armenia and Azerbaijan declare their independence (May). Lenin shot by Dora Kaplan (August).

1921   Eighth Party Congress in March. The introduction of the New Economic Policy. Lenin's illness begins.

1922   Lenin's health worsens. Stalin appointed General Secretary of the Communist Party.

1924   The death of Lenin (21 January).

The Reputation

Lenin was born Vladimir Ilyich Ulyanov. Lenin was the name he adopted when he became a revolutionary.

Before 1914 Leningrad was called St Petersburg, after its founder, Peter the Great. In 1915 the German name was changed to Petrograd and, on Lenin's death, in 1924, to Leningrad.

Red Flag: the flag of revolution, adopted by the Communists.

Crowds queuing to visit Lenin's mausoleum in Red Square.

A Western visitor to the Soviet Union today is quickly made aware of the name Vladimir Ilyich Lenin. His portrait is prominently displayed, as are many quotations from his books. His name has been given to an underground station, the major Soviet library and numerous roads. Even Russia's second largest city was renamed Leningrad in his honour.

Walking through Moscow's Red Square, one sees long queues of people waiting in a patient and orderly fashion outside a large, square building made of red marble, which stands just below the wall of the Kremlin, the medieval fortress where the present-day government resides. This is the mausoleum, holding, in an illuminated glass case, the embalmed body of Lenin. It is worth reflecting on the fact that far, far more people have seen Lenin dead than ever saw him alive.

On another day one may visit a school. In each classroom one will see Lenin's portrait, while at the end of the hall there is likely to be a 'Lenin corner', in which a portrait or bust of Lenin is displayed with the Red Flag, surrounded by flowers. Numerous songs refer to him. An American visitor heard the following at a kindergarten in Soviet Central Asia:

In many countries children live,
And everywhere all children love Lenin.

An English lesson at a school in Ashkhabad.

Who then is this man who – though he died in 1924 – is still revered today? This book will try to explain his importance through a study of his life and the major events with which he was concerned. Various points of view will be put forward – some in the form of quotations from Lenin himself, or from his friends and compatriots, and others in the form of quotations from historians writing after his death. You will soon come to realize that the facts of Lenin's life are rarely in dispute; differences arise, rather, in the selection of material and in the emphasis given to it.

Another theme which will become apparent is that people's attitudes towards the past change over time. It is thus essential to check *when* and *where* a book was first published, and to find out something about the author. If he was a contemporary of Lenin was he a supporter or was he in opposition? Like Trotsky, he may even have been forced into exile.

Naturally, Lenin is a figure about whom writers and observers have strongly disagreed, often at great length. Indeed, more words have probably been written about Lenin than any other twentieth-century politician. In 1914 Charles Rappaport, a Russo-French socialist who later became an important Communist, wrote of him:

'No party could exist under the regime of this Social Democratic tsar, who regards

Trotsky: a Communist theorist who played a major part in the Russian Revolution; deported from Russia by Stalin in 1929. See p. 62.

Communist: a believer in the ideals of Karl Marx and Friedrich Engels; a card-carrying member of the Communist Party. See p. 10.

himself as a super-Marxist but who is, in reality, nothing but an adventurer of the highest order.'

Before 1917 many socialists – Russians as well as non-Russians – saw Lenin's insistence that he alone knew the best way forward as a threat to the revolutionary movement. After 1917 the views of left-wingers tended to change. Trotsky, writing in the year of Lenin's death, described him as 'the engine driver of history' – one who made things happen. A British I.L.P. Socialist, James Maxton, likewise said:

i) At critical periods he had to stand alone, his friends aloof. Few of the men who started on the road with him finished the course by his side. He set too hot a pace. He demanded more sacrifices than most men were ready to give.
ii) One looks through history in vain to find someone with whom comparison is possible.
iii) In political life there have been more subtle statesmen. But nowhere is to be found in any single man the peculiar combination of devotion, courage, wisdom, skill and human understanding except in the man Lenin . . . .

(James Maxton, *Lenin*, 1932)

Might the author's political allegiance make his judgment on Lenin unreliable?

From 1917 to 1934 the Central Committee was a form of Parliament. By 1939 Stalin had liquidated 70% of its members, considerably reducing its powers.

Soviet troops prepare for May Day in Leningrad.

Lenin himself encouraged propaganda, and in 1920 the Central Committee of the Communist Party established 'Agitprop', the Department of Agitation and Propaganda. Even before this, Lenin had realized the potential of propaganda, and speeches and the written word were supplemented by street theatrics, festivals, paintings, badges, flags, banners, statues and busts, all aimed at getting the Communist message across to the people. Hard-working workers and peasants represented what is good; their enemies were the foreign powers, the landlords and the

Capitalist: usually refers to one who has money and employs others, or who gains income from investments. Communists usually refer to Western democracies as capitalist.

Pravda, meaning 'Truth' is the daily newspaper of the Communist Party. *Soldatskaya Pravda* was the soldiers' edition.

capitalists, as well as former tsarists and non-Communist parties and groups. May Day became the great revolutionary public holiday, and the successful 1917 revolution is still celebrated each October with huge march pasts in Red Square and throughout the Soviet Union.

Lenin allowed his own name to be used in the service of the State. In November 1917 a soldiers' newspaper, *Soldatskaya Pravda*, published a poem dedicated to Lenin:

. . . Hail to you, our leader of the people,
  Champion of rights and ideas,
  Pure as crystal, noble,
  The terror of the rich and of tsars!
  The families of workers, of the hungry
  Are in your ranks – your shield in battle:
  Their legion of sons of the free
  Is on guard – believes – will triumph.
(Quoted in N. Tumarkin, *Lenin Lives!*, 1983.)

Soon Lenin was being described in even more high-flown terms. On the sixth anniversary of the Revolution, on 7 November 1923, *Pravda* wrote:

Lenin is not only the name of a beloved leader; it is a programme and a tactic . . .
Lenin is the rule of pure reason . . .
Lenin . . . is the rejection of all compromises, of all half-measures . . .
Lenin is a limitless enthusiasm for science and technology . . .
In Lenin . . . all problems find a solution . . .
Lenin is . . . a fight against a whole world of enemies armed to the teeth . . .
Lenin . . . is the one Communist Party of the Red Globe.
Long live Comrade Lenin!
(Quoted in N. Tumarkin, *Lenin Lives!*)

In what ways has this portrayal of Lenin moved a stage further?

During his lifetime Lenin portrayed himself as a man of the people, who even delayed meetings with foreign leaders so that he could talk with workers. At the Tenth Congress of the Communist Party in 1921 Lenin filled in a questionnaire which is evidence of his commitment to his work:

Date of birth: 1870.
Condition of health: Well.
What languages do you know? English; German; French poorly; Italian very poorly.
What localities in Russia do you know well and how long did you live in them? I know the Volga region, where I was born and raised until 17 years of age.
What All Russian Congresses did you attend? All except the July or August [Congresses], 1917
Were you abroad? In a number of countries of Western Europe in 1895, 1900-1905, 1908-1917.
Military training: None.
Education: Graduated in 1891 from the Law Faculty of Petrograd University.
Basic occupation up to 1917: Literary.
What are your specialities? None.
What did you do after 1917 outside Party, trade union, soviet, etc. work? In addition to the above, only literary work.
What union are you a member of at the present time? The Union of Journalists.
Work from 1917: Chairman of the Council of People's Commissars and of the Council of Labour and Defence.
How long have you been a member of the Communist Party? Since 1894.
Did you belong to other parties, and, if so, to which? No.
Participation in the revolutionary movement:

WHEN	WHERE	IN WHAT ORGANIZATION?
1892-1893	Samara	Illegal circles of Social-Democrats and a

1894-1895	Petersburg	member of the Russian Social-Democratic
1895-1897	Prison	Labour Party from its foundation.
1898-1900	Yenisey Province	
1900-1905	Abroad	
1905-1907	Petersburg	
1908-1817	Abroad	

Were you persecuted for revolutionary activity? Arrested, 1887; arrested, 1895-1897; Siberia, 1898-1900; arrested, 1900.

How long were you in prison? 14 months and a few days.

Penal servitude or exile: 3 years.

In exile abroad: 9-10 years.

(Quoted in J. Stalin, *Lenin*, 1934)

After Lenin's death in January 1924 many memories were stirred. One writer recalled a visit made by Lenin to Kashino in 1920, marking the bringing of electricity to the village:

Astounding – such a person, and he has no gold ring, no chain, no gold watch . . . astounding!

(Quoted in N. Tumarkin, *Lenin Lives!*)

A statue of Lenin in the Kremlin, Moscow.

But Lenin also had, and still has, his critics. The leading Russian playwright Maxim Gorky, writing in the newspaper *Novaya Zhizn* ('New Life'), portrayed him in a very different light:

Cohorts: troops.

Lenin, Trotsky and their cohorts are already intoxicated with the poison of power, as is proved by their shameful attitude towards freedom of speech, personal liberty, and that group of rights for which democracy has struggled . . . Lenin and his acolytes believe themselves entitled to commit every crime . . .
(Quoted in Victor Serge, *From Lenin to Stalin*, 1937)

Acolytes: followers.

While Gorky represents a very different view of Lenin is there any way in which his views complement or add to those of the previous writers?

Maiakovsky wrote many poems about the Revolution, but became disenchanted with the Party and committed suicide in 1930. What was his objection to the advertisement? How does he wish to see Lenin remembered?

The poet Maiakovsky, writing after Lenin's death in 1924, strongly objected to the following advertisement:

BUSTS
OF V.I. LENIN
plaster, treated copper, bronze,
marble, granite.
LIFE-SIZED AND DOUBLE LIFE-SIZED
from the original approved for reproduction
and distribution by the commission on the
Immortalization
OF THE MEMORY OF V.I. LENIN

Maiakovsky replied in verse:

We are against this.
We agree with the railroad workers from the Kazan RR who asked an artist to decorate the Lenin hall in their club without busts and portraits of Lenin, saying: 'We don't want icons.'
We insist:
Don't mechanically punch out Lenin.
Don't print his portraits on posters, on tablecloths, on plates, on mugs, on cigarette-cases . . .
Lenin is still our contemporary.
He is among the living.
We need him alive, and not dead.
Therefore,
Learn from Lenin, but don't canonize him.
(Quoted in N. Tumarkin, *Lenin Lives!*)

Joseph Stalin became General Secretary of the Communist Party in 1922 and went on to rule through a reign of terror. See p. 60.

Party: refers to the Communist Party. This was never intended to be a mass party, and its members are carefully selected.

Bear this argument in mind as you read the rest of this book and try to decide whether or not it is justified.

One of the main criticisms made of Lenin by non-Communist Russians and many Western historians is that he laid the foundations of the terrible 'Stalin years' of the 1930s, during which the régime murdered many millions of Soviet citizens. This view is expressed by Leonard Schapiro, writing in 1983:

It was by means of the Party machine Lenin had forged that Stalin rose to power in the [1920s] . . . . It was by exploitation of Lenin's system of Communist control that Stalin established his mastery over the country . . . it was from Lenin that Stalin inherited the instruments of rule; and once provided with the means, Stalin was as unlikely as Lenin to be restrained by moral considerations . . .
L. Schapiro, *1917*, 1983)

USSR: the Union of Soviet Socialist Republics, the name given in 1922 to present-day Russia, which comprises the Russian republic and 14 others.

This book will present the main episodes in Lenin's life in such a way as to enable you to understand why he has such an extraordinary reputation in the USSR today. It will also help you to appreciate why many non-Communists have reservations about him.

The Background

Our epoch, the epoch of the bourgeoisie . . . has simplified the class antagonisms.

Bourgeoisie: originally meant town-dwellers, but now refers to the middle classes.

Proletariat: The wage-earners of the towns and cities.

Friedrich Engels (1820-95) was a businessman and friend of Marx. On his retirement he devoted his time to revolutionary writings.

The history of all hitherto existing society is the history of class struggles.

Our epoch, the epoch of the bourgeoisie . . . has simplified the class antagonisms. Society as a whole is more and more splitting up into two great hostile camps . . . Bourgeoisie and Proletariat.

. . . the bourgeoisie . . . produces . . . its own grave-diggers. Its fall and the victory of the proletariat are equally inevitable.

The Communists declare . . . that their ends can be attained only by the forcible overthrow of all existing social conditions. Let the ruling class tremble at a Communistic revolution. The proletarians have nothing to lose but their chains. They have a world to win. Working men of all countries unite!
(Karl Marx and Friedrich Engels, *The Communist Manifesto*, 1848.)

These brief extracts are from the *Communist Manifesto*, co-written by the German revolutionary and philosopher of Communism, Karl Marx. First published in 1848, the extracts pinpoint some of Marx's key ideas, without some understanding of which Lenin's life makes little sense, since he was a student and interpreter of Marxism, and the founder of the world's first Communist state.

Marx wrote many books (the most famous is *Capital*, published in 1867), as well as pamphlets and newspaper articles, over a period of 40 years. It

Early editions of the Communist Manifesto *and* Capital. *Both of these works are still frequently reprinted. Why do you think that part of the title page of the* Communist Manifesto *was printed in French?*

is not easy, therefore, to reduce his beliefs to a paragraph. Essentially, however, Marx believed from his study of history that it was possible to predict the future. (This is why Marxism is sometimes described as 'scientific'.) Marx saw the past, present and future as a continual struggle for power. First the nobles challenged the authority of the king. Then they in turn found themselves threatened by the growing power of the middle classes (the capitalist owners of factories and banks). According to Marx the third stage in this inevitable process would come when the proletariat had grown in numbers and strength to the extent that they could seize power from the bourgeoisie. When they had succeeded in doing so the class struggle would cease, since there would now be only one class, and during a period of time of indeterminate length (which Marx called the 'dictatorship of the proletariat') the transformation of society along Communist lines would start. There would be no private property; the state would own the means of production, distribution and exchange. Thus there would no longer be the exploitation of the workers by those who owned the means of production (the factories, machinery, and so on). Education and medical care would be provided free by the state. Ultimately, Marx believed, the disciplinary framework of the state would wither away and a sort of paradise on earth – the Communist society – would exist. All would co-operate willingly and share happily and fairly the abundance of material goods.

Marx, who died in 1883, expected the Communist revolution to take place first in countries like Britain and Germany, where industrialization was proceeding rapidly during his lifetime, creating a discontented urban working class. This was not true of Russia, which Marx frequently spoke of contemptuously, remarking on one occasion that the USA was more likely to see a Communist revolution than Russia!

Marx had such a low estimate of Russia's readiness for revolution because of her political and economic backwardness. Ruled by the all-powerful tsar, a member of the Romanov family, Russia had no Parliament, and her ministers were no more than advisers. The tsar was supported by the Russian Orthodox Church, which along with the tsar and the nobility held most of Russia's land.

Tsar: ruler of Russia, from the Latin *Caesar*, meaning 'emperor'.

A village outside Moscow, taken before 1914. Notice the unpaved road. What season do you think this photograph was taken in?

Serfdom: condition in which a person's service is attached to the land on which they work, and transferred with it. A form of slavery.

Tsar Alexander II was known as the 'Tsar Liberator'. He was assassinated in 1881.

The Far Eastern War, it was hoped, would divert attention from Russia's internal problems. Instead, defeat and loss of life made these problems worse.

Duma: an elected assembly granted by the tsar. Its powers were limited, and its members drawn from only a small part of the population. It often clashed with the tsar.

In 1901 Ulyanov began using the pseudonym 'Lenin', derived from the River Lena.

Valentinov was also known as Volsky. See p. 18.

Autocratic regime: one in which the ruler has total power. Even after the granting of the October Manifesto in 1905 the tsar retained the title 'autocrat'.

Can you think of any political beliefs today that would attract young people in a similar fashion?

In Marx's lifetime the vast majority of Russia's population were peasants who worked on the land. Only in 1861 did the tsar free them from serfdom, giving them land, which they had to pay the state for over a period of 49 years. Russia's population grew rapidly in the last quarter of the nineteenth century, and faced with insufficient land to cultivate, many peasants moved to the towns. Consequently, cities like St Petersburg and Moscow grew rapidly. At the same time, and especially in the 1890s, the state encouraged industrialization as a means of allowing Russia to move with the times and remain a great power. By 1900 conditions in the towns for the workers were appalling, and in the countryside, where the vast majority of people still lived, hardship and sometimes famine continued. Russia was a nation striving to modernize, but she was still ruled by a tsar with feudal powers.

When Russia was defeated by Japan in the Far Eastern War of 1904-5 a revolution followed, forcing Tsar Nicholas II to make some changes. A Parliament, the Duma, was established, and the peasants were freed from making any more repayments for their land. By 1914 agriculture was becoming more productive and some peasants were prosperous enough to employ others as labourers.

Marx's views on revolution and the proletariat were known to some educated Russians, members of the 'intelligentsia', from the start of the 1870s, but many revolutionaries in Russia at this time believed that it was only by converting the *peasants* to socialism that revolution in Russia would occur. The peasants, however, showed no interest in this vision, and, consequently, one group of disaffected revolutionaries turned to the weapon of assassination. In 1881 they killed Tsar Alexander II and thereafter many Russian revolutionaries sought safety in Western Europe. In the mid-1880s a Marxist group under George Plekhanov was set up in Switzerland. He argued that Russia was not yet ready for socialism, and that she had first to pass through the capitalist stage – the second of the three historical stages identified by Marx. This argument was supported at the end of the 1890s by younger men within Russia, of whom one of the most important was V.I. Ulyanov.

Lenin was born Vladimir Ilyich Ulyanov in Simbirsk in 1870. He was from a well-to-do family – his father was director of schools for the region. However, in 1887 Lenin's elder brother was executed for plotting to assassinate the tsar. When news of his hanging reached the Ulyanov family it is said that Lenin cried 'I'll make them pay for this! I swear it!' Lenin went to university, where he studied law, but was expelled for his involvement in a student demonstration. By the time Lenin finally graduated in 1891 he had become a Marxist. He believed that the way forward was not by terror and assassination but rather by patient propaganda amongst the growing number of industrial workers in Russia, showing them that as Russia developed she would go through the stages of development identified by Marx, ultimately becoming a socialist state.

Nikolay Valentinov, another young revolutionary – and later a colleague of Lenin, explained the attractions of Marxism to men of their type:

We seized on Marxism because we were attracted by its . . . optimism, its strong belief . . . that . . . the development of capitalism . . . was creating new social forces . . . which would sweep away the autocratic régime together with its abominations . . . . Marxism . . . was new, and fresh and exciting.
(Quoted in R. Conquest, *Lenin*, 1972)

In 1893, Lenin moved to St Petersburg, where he worked as a lawyer, studied Marx, wrote pamphlets and tried to spread the Marxist message

The Ulyanov family. Lenin is in the front row on the right.

among the factory workers there. In 1895, Lenin and another revolutionary, Yuly Martov, united the various Marxist groups in the capital into the League of Struggle for the Emancipation of the Working Classes. At the end of the year, Lenin was arrested with most of the other members and imprisoned for 14 months before being exiled to Siberia. Freed in 1900, he made his way to Switzerland.

The first years of the new century were a lean period for revolutionaries like Lenin. Exiled in capitalist Western Europe, in Raymond Pearson's words, 'they expended their surplus energy on the only exercise to which their predicament allowed recourse – party polemics [arguments]'. At the time of the 1905 revolution in Russia, Lenin was in Geneva. By now he was the leader of his own small party, but he did not return to Russia until November 1905, by which time he could only witness the final defeat of the revolution from the sidelines.

Some historians argue strongly that by 1914 the tsarist autocracy had been modified and that it was likely that Russia would turn gradually into a liberal constitutional monarchy. Be that as it may, the prospects for the revolutionaries seemed poor. They were divided amongst themselves and

The liberal constitutional monarchy envisaged was one where the Duma would have much more power and the country would thus be ruled by a form of parliamentary government.

The founders of the Union of the Struggle for the Liberation of the Working Classes, St Petersburg 1895. Lenin is sitting behind the table, with Martov on his left.

Until February 1918, Russia followed the calendar established by Julius Caesar (the Julian Calendar). By the nineteenth century the rest of Europe had adopted the more accurate Gregorian calendar introduced by Pope Gregory XIII in 1582. By 1918 the Russian Calendar was 13 days behind that of the West. In this book, to avoid confusion, the Western dating system has been used. The first revolution thus began on 8 March rather than 23 February, and the Bolshevik coup took place on the night of 6/7 November rather than 24/5 October.

Bolsheviks: break-away group of the Russian Social Democratic Labour party, under Lenin. Formed in 1903.

The New Economic Policy, introduced in 1921, allowed limited trading and the re-opening of markets.

their ranks were infiltrated by the Okhrana (the tsar's secret police). The outbreak of the First World War in 1914 transformed the situation. A relatively small-scale war in 1904-5 had produced domestic turmoil; the unprecedented scale and duration of the 1914-17 war had an even greater effect on Russia.

Revolution took place in March 1917. It was caused by the failure of the government to cope with the demands of total war. Prices had risen sharply and food was in short supply. Protests and bread riots in Petrograd turned into revolution. The army, which had remained loyal to the tsar in 1905, now either supported the rioters or stood aside. Tsar Nicholas II was soon forced to abdicate.

Lenin returned to Russia in April 1917 and it is largely due to his personality, his organization and his drive that a second revolution took place in November, giving Lenin's supporters, the Bolsheviks, control of the country. Lenin took Russia out of the war against Germany in March 1918, but was soon fighting a civil war which the Bolsheviks only won after Russia had undergone terrible suffering. In March 1921, Lenin realized that concessions had to be made in order to get the country back on its feet and to ensure that the Communist Party (as the Bolsheviks were now called) retained power. Thus a limited degree of private enterprise in industry – the New Economic Policy – was introduced.

Three years later, Lenin died. He had worked relentlessly in the cause of his political beliefs, but he never fully recovered from an assassination attempt in 1918. The rest of this book will assess Lenin's reputation and will focus on his work between 1900 and 1924.

Interpretations

The Parliamentary or the Revolutionary Road to Socialism?

At the very start of the twentieth century, socialists in Europe were divided. In 1899, a German socialist, Edward Bernstein, published a book called *Evolutionary Socialism*. Robert Conquest describes Bernstein's essential ideas:

It was an assertion that Marx had, in certain respects, made a faulty analysis of the whole course of events in the West . . . wages had not gone down . . . there was no sign of the predicted capitalist failure to expand production . . . revolutionary situations had not arisen. He concluded that Marx was in error about the inevitable economic dead end of capitalism, and that it now appeared that wealth could gradually become more diffused and a peaceful transition to socialism be achieved.
(R. Conquest, *Lenin*).

The German Social Democratic Party (S.P.D.) was the largest socialist party in the world at this time. Officially, the party was revolutionary and Marxist; in fact it was becoming increasingly respectable – by 1912 it had 110 seats in the Reichstag, the German parliament, and was the largest party.

It was clear to Bernstein that the Marxist course of events was not developing as planned. He wrote that: 'every kopek increase in wages, every hour less in the working day, brings us nearer to the socialist future'. But the leaders of the S.P.D. would not give up their belief in the necessity of revolution, and Bernstein was bitterly attacked.

In the same year a young Russian, Katherine Kushova, drew up a document known as the *Credo*. According to B.D. Wolfe, Kuskova declared that:

The general law of labour activity . . . was for the movement to follow 'the path of least resistance'. In the West, where the bourgeoisie had conquered political rights for itself and for the proletariat, the working class had found it easier to go into politics than to build [trade] unions. But in Russia, where the tsar represented a stone wall blocking political action, the path of least resistance was economic action against the employers and the attempt to organize trade unions. The Russian working class was too weak and backward for politics.
(B.D. Wolfe, *Three Men Who Made a Revolution*, 1948).

Lenin responded harshly to this view. His first editorial in *Iskra* is paraphrased by Adam Ulam:

Any socialist party worthy of its name must lead the masses and must instruct them as to where their real interests lie. The masses may want to slacken in their march

Kopek: a small Russian coin.

Why would Lenin regard Bernstein as such a threat to his hopes?

Iskra: the 'spark'. The newspaper of the Russian Social Democratic Labour Party, founded in Switzerland in 1900 and smuggled into Russia.

The first edition of Iskra, *printed in Switzerland in 1900. Do you think the title (meaning 'spark') was a good one?*

How does Lenin's argument differ from that of Bernstein?.

Revisionism: the modification of Marx's ideas. Today the word would also imply a modification of Lenin's thinking.

Lenin went on to say that the role of the Party was to lead the workers towards revolution. How real do you think Lenin's fear was? In the second paragraph, what qualities is Lenin demanding from a revolutionary?

towards revolution, to content themselves with economic concessions; the party must urge them on . . . .
(A.B. Ulam, *Lenin and the Bolsheviks*, 1965)

To Lenin, the ideas of Bernstein and Kuskova seemed to strip socialism of its revolutionary meaning, turning it into a sort of middle-class 'do-goodism'. Their ideas also called into question his work of the previous ten years. Lenin feared that if the ideas of 'revisionists' like Bernstein, and 'economists' like Kuskova, took hold then the workers would lose their revolutionary will. He responded, therefore, with the pamphlet *What is to be Done?*, published in 1902:

The history of all countries shows that the working class, exclusively by its own effort, is able to develop only trade union consciousness, i.e., it may itself realise the necessity for combining in unions, to fight against the employers and to strive to compel the government to pass necessary labour legislation . . . . A Social Democrat must not be afraid of long work. He must work and work without leaving off. He must be ever ready to do anything – whether it be to save the honour, prestige and pre-eminence of the Party at the time of the greatest revolutionary 'depression', or whether it be to prepare, plan and carry out a nationwide armed uprising.
(Lenin, *What is to be done?*, 1902.)

Thus, according to Lenin, to bring about a revolution a genuinely revolutionary party was needed – one 'embracing primarily and chiefly people whose profession consists of revolutionary activity'. Full-time revolutionaries had to encourage the workers in the factories to fight against their employers, until their anger sparked off a mass strike of the population. Then the tsar and all his works would be removed and a new government would promote and implement socialism.

Professional Revolutionaries or a Mass Party?

The Russian Social Democratic Party was founded at a congress held in Minsk in 1898. However, as only nine delegates attended, and they were arrested a few weeks later, the effective establishment of the party took place at a series of meetings held in Brussels and London in 1903. At the

22nd session, devoted to a definition of party membership, Lenin proposed that:

A Party member accepts the Party Programme, supports the Party financially and must belong to one of its organizations.

This was amended by Martov:

A member need not belong to a Party organization but can work under the direction of one of them.
(Quoted in Anon, *Lenin for Beginners*, 1977)

The amendment was carried by 28 votes to 23. Modern Communist sources stress:

Sharp differences of opinion were revealed at the Congress during the discussion on Party Rules. Lenin was for a monolith militant party, every member of which would take an active part in the revolutionary struggle and submit to Party discipline. He therefore maintained that anyone who accepted the Party Programme, paid his dues, belonged to one of its organizations and participated in its work, could be considered a member of the Party.
(Anon, *Lenin: A Short Biography*, 1979)

Volsky was the pseudonym of Valentinov. At first a great admirer of Lenin, he later broke with him and lived most of his life in exile in Paris.

Volsky, however, a contemporary of Lenin whose work has never been published in Russia, recalls how Lenin replied to his question on the differences of 18 January 1904:

In substance there are no great differences of principle. The only disagreement at all of this order is of paragraph 1 of the party rules . . . . But this is a very unimportant disagreement. It is not a matter of life and death for the Party . . . . I was left in the minority, but neither I nor the others who supported me had any thoughts whatever about causing a split.
(N.V. Volsky, *Encounters with Lenin*, 1968)

Lenin recounted a discussion with a 'Centre', middle-of-the-road delegate:

'What a depressing atmosphere prevails at our Congress,' he complained to me. 'All this fierce fighting, this agitation one against the other, these sharp polemics [arguments], this uncomradely attitude!' – what a fine thing our Congress is,' I replied to him, 'opportunity for open fighting. Opinions expressed. Tendencies revealed. Groups defined. Hands raised. A decision taken. A stage passed through. Forward! That's what I like! That's life!' . . . . The comrade of the 'Centre' looked on me as though perplexed, and shrugged his shoulders. We had spoken in different languages.
(N.K. Krupskaya, *Memories of Lenin*, 1930)

Divisions occurred over the Party newspaper, *Iskra*, and the membership of the editorial board, which would give its members power over the Party.

By the time the vote took place, several delegates had walked out and Lenin's group won. From this time on the victors were known as the 'Bolsheviks' (the Russian word for 'majority') and the losers as the 'Mensheviks'. Georgy Plekhanov, often regarded as the founder of Russian Marxism, was more worried about the split than Lenin, and he invited several of the defeated group to rejoin the *Iskra* board. At this point Lenin resigned and founded his own newspaper, *Vyperod* in December 1904.

Lenin's determination is vividly portrayed by Volsky:

It became quite obvious from what Lenin was saying that the right to the

Mensheviks: from the Russian word for 'minority'. The smaller group at the 1903 conferences.

conductor's baton inside the Party could only belong to him . . . . For Lenin this was simply a matter which required no proof . . . . Adherence to Bolshevism seemed somehow to imply a kind of oath of loyalty to Lenin, a vow to follow his lead unquestioningly . . . every argument on Party matters began and ended with the question of Lenin.
(N.V. Volsky, *Encounters with Lenin*)

Why should we be cautious about Volsky as a witness? Why is he still important? (See p. 18.)

The Mensheviks saw Lenin's supporters as a set of puppets who were there only to carry out Lenin's orders. To them, as Volsky wrote, he was 'conceited, intolerant, power loving, rude, quarrelsome and tactless'.

How do you explain the Menshevik view of Lenin? Does it contradict the earlier comments, or add to them?

Lenin spent most of 1905, when Russia was in the midst of revolution, far away in Switzerland. He was not idle, however. He read all he could on military tactics and civil war; he scoured the notes of Marx; he read widely on the 1848 revolutions in Europe. He also interviewed individuals coming out of Russia, received letters and messages and kept himself thoroughly up to date on developments there. He only travelled to Russia, however, after the tsar issued his 'October Manifesto' in 1905, which granted civil liberty and freedom of speech. From St Petersburg Lenin watched the bitter fighting in Moscow in December 1905 – the last-ditch stand of the revolution. If the Bolsheviks had played little part in the events in St Petersburg, during the winter of 1905, 'the moral responsibility', in the words of B.D. Wolfe, 'if not the direct initiative, was above all Lenin's and that of his party' (B.D. Wolfe, *Three Who Made a Revolution*, 1948). After all, from the start of 1905 Lenin had urged the necessity of an armed uprising. An American eyewitness recounts how barricades were set up in working-class areas of Moscow:

1848 was the year when revolution broke out in many European countries. By 1850 all these uprisings had been suppressed.

The barricades were never intended to be 'fought'. The only tactic of the revolutionists were ambush and surprise . . . . By the side-street barricades and wire-entanglements they had rid themselves of the fear of cavalry. By the barricades across the main streets, they rendered the approach of troops necessarily slow.
(H.W. Nevinson, *The Dawn in Russia*, 1906)

Defeat was only a matter of time, despite fierce resistance from the 'revolutionists'.

Although the Moscow uprising was unsuccessful, it was important to the revolutionaries, as Nevinson comments:

The failure at Moscow fell like a blight upon all Russia, and hope withered. The revolutionists, certainly, protested that much was gained. They admitted that they had allowed their hand to be forced by the Government. The attempt, they knew, was ill-timed and ill-devised but they had not intended to win this time; the rising was only a dress rehearsal for the great revolution hereafter. They were teaching the proletariat the methods of street fighting, and after all it was something to have held a large part of the ancient capital for ten days against the Government troops. Such a thing had never been accomplished before.
(H.W. Nevinson, *The Dawn in Russia*)

Why do you think that the 1905 revolution was bound to end in failure?

Lenin would have agreed with these sentiments but he nonetheless felt that the rising indicated some of the weaknesses of the revolutionaries' organization:

What offensive tactics could have been adopted? How would you have looked back on the Moscow uprising if you had taken part?

He pointed out that arms should have been taken up more resolutely, that offensive and not defensive action should have been waged, that the troops should have been won over and the peasants drawn into the common struggle.
(Anon, *Lenin: A Short Biography*)

Two differing views of the 1905 revolution. How can you tell which is in support of the revolution and which against?

Admiral Dubassov was the officer who led the tsarist forces in Moscow.

Why did Lenin believe that the guns revolutionized the masses?

To quote Lenin directly:

Dubassov's guns have revolutionized new masses of the people to an unprecedented degree . . . . 'What now? We will look reality straight in the face.' (Quoted in N.K. Krupskaya, *Memories of Lenin*)

Lenin was once again forced into exile.

A modern poster commemorating the 1905 revolution.

Prague was then within the Austro-Hungarian Empire.

The Bolshevik conference at Prague in 1910 marked the final breach with the Mensheviks. The issue which first provoked the split in the Russian Social Democratic Labour Party in 1903 might seem a mere quibble, but it turned out to symbolize deeper differences in the R.S.D.L.P. ranks. After 1910 it was clear that the Bolsheviks and Mensheviks envisaged two quite different kinds of revolution. The Mensheviks believed that Russia had to become a bourgeois parliamentary republic before the working class could seize power – and this last event might be far in the future. Lenin was by now more impatient. He wanted to telescope the two revolutions together by encouraging the peasants to revolt against the landowning nobility, and thus, acting as the allies of the industrial working class, carry out their socialist revolution against the capitalists. Although Lenin's thoughts on this matter were not fully worked out until 1917, one of the lessons he learnt from the events of 1905 was that success would have been more likely with a strong worker-peasant alliance.

Worker: in this context means 'industrial worker', a member of the proletariat.

The years after 1905 were depressing for the revolutionaries. Many of their leaders were in prison or in exile; money for propaganda was in short supply; and in Russia, under the guidance of Prime Minister Peter Stolypin, agriculture and industry were developing rapidly. Then, in 1911, Stolypin was assassinated. The government responded with a clamp-down, giving the revolutionary movement the spur it needed. In 1912 a wave of strikes spread throughout Russia. When soldiers shot 250 gold workers on the Lena River in Siberia, Lenin interpreted the situation:

The shots on the Lena, have broken the lie of silence, and the torrent of the people's movement has been unleashed.
(Quoted in Anon, *Lenin: A Short Biography*)

In 1913, 850,000 workers went on strike; in the first few months of 1914 this

Franz Ferdinand and his wife were assassinated in Sarajevo, capital of the province of Bosnia.

figure rose to 2 million. In the years 1912-14 Lenin alone wrote 280 articles for the new Bolshevik newspaper, *Pravda*. Then, on 28 June 1914, the heir to the Austro-Hungarian throne was assassinated, and within six weeks Russia and her allies, France and Britain, had been drawn into the First World War against Germany and Austria-Hungary.

Defence of the Motherland or Imperialist War?

Russia at war

On the outbreak of war Lenin saw that events in Russia were developing in favour of revolution, so he moved to Cracow in Austria-Hungary, to be nearer to the Russian border. However, he was arrested there and fled back to neutral Switzerland. Alexander Solzhenitsyn, the Russian dissident historian and novelist, imagines the tedious and frustrating life of Lenin as a revolutionary in exile:

Dissident: a person disagreeing with the views of the established government of his or her country.

> But these last ten years, since his second emigration, had been filled, stuffed, packed tight with – what? Nothing but paper – envelopes, packets, newspaper wrappers, routine letters, express letters – so much time went on correspondence alone . . . . Almost his whole life, half of every day, went into those endless letters. Nobody lived near him, his sympathisers were scattered to the four corners of the earth, and from a distance he had to keep their loyalty, rally, direct, advise, interrogate, beg, and thank them . . . .
> (A. Solzhenitsyn, *Lenin in Zurich*, 1976)

What do you think are the major qualities required of a revolutionary leader in exile?

It is important to remember that this is a novel, although it is based on fact.

Once again the revolutionaries argued among themselves. Many felt that they should fight as Russians against Germany. Lenin was outraged at the news that socialist parties throughout Europe – parties which had always preached the unity of the international working class – were now in 1914 rushing to support their individual governments and fight each other.

Some revolutionaries felt that they should fight for peace, but Lenin took a different view. He told the Zimmerwald Conference of European Anti-War Socialists in 1915 that:

> The working masses had to organize and prepare for a decisive fight with the bourgeoisie, [and] prepare for civil war.

'The Call to the Flag.' A British postcard from Christmas 1915 incorporating the names of the Allies.

To this end Lenin put forward the slogan:

Why was Lenin taking a risk in putting forward such a slogan?

'Work for the defeat of your own government in the imperialist war.'
(Quoted in Anon, *Lenin: A Short Biography*)

Lenin's view was not that of the majority, however, and at Kienthal in April 1916 his view remained unpopular:

Sectarian: a person with strict, rigidly held beliefs.

Most of the Western Socialist leaders looked upon him, anyhow, as a fanatical, romantic revolutionary sectarian.
(G. von Rauch, *A History of Soviet Russia*, 1967)

By contrast the official Communist Party view today is that:

At this crucial moment in history Lenin, with the Bolshevik Party he had created and reared, held high the banner of proletarian internationalism. Lenin's courageous call to declare war on the war resounded throughout the world.
(Anon, *Lenin: A Short Biography*)

In what way do these two views differ?

Many had expected that the war would be over by Christmas 1914, but soon there was stalemate on the Western Front, while in the east the Russians, after initial successes, suffered heavy losses in the face of both Austrian and German troops. Throughout the war the Russians remained crucially isolated from their western allies.

Imperialism: the belief in the desirability of acquiring colonies, and extending a country's influence through trade and diplomacy.

It was important that Lenin should seek to explain the true nature of the war, and to this end he published, in 1916, *Imperialism: the Highest Stage of Capitalism*. In this work Lenin argued that the war had been caused by capitalism and that it was, therefore, not the concern of the working people. He argued that while countries such as Britain, France and Germany had seen an improvement in the living standards of working people, capitalism was essentially self-destructive and that in its higher stage – imperialism – it had led to war. Lenin argued in more detail, that with the imperialist stage, when European countries had sought overseas empires and acquired territories in Asia and Africa, quarrels had developed over territory and war had ensued.

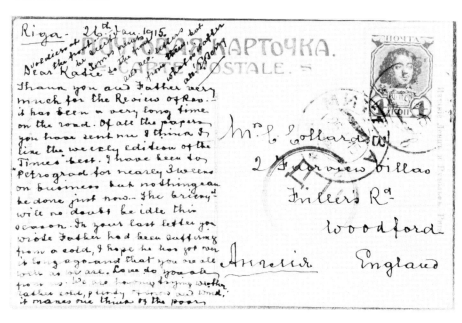

A British postcard from Riga. Notice the censor's stamp, and the reference to 'the soldiers at the front'.

Lenin was constantly involved in arguments and discussions at this time. Solzhenitsyn imagines his mood in 1916:

He was nearing the end of his forty-seventh year, in an anxious, monotonous life of nothing but ink on paper, emnities and alliances, quarrels and agreements that sprang up and faded in a day or a week.
(A. Solzhenitsyn, *Lenin in Zurich*)

Lenin's wife, in her memoirs, recalled:

Never, I think, was Vladimir Ilyich in a more irreconcilable mood than during the last months of 1916 and the early months of 1917.
(N.K. Krupskaya, *Memories of Lenin*)

The March Revolution

The outbreak of the February Revolution in Petrograd in March 1917 took everyone, including the revolutionaries, by surprise. Leon Trotsky (who had played a leading role in the 1905 revolution) had gone to the USA in December 1916, convinced that he was seeing Europe for the last time. In January 1917 Lenin gave a lecture to Swiss students, ending with the words:

We of the older generation may not see the decisive battles of this coming revolution.
(Quoted in R. Conquest, *Lenin*, 1972)

At this time Lenin's name was only vaguely known in Russia and usually suggested an excitable revolutionary who, many believed, was out of touch with the real world of Russia.

By 15 March 1917 the tsar had abdicated and Russia had become a republic. A temporary Provisional Government was formed by liberal members of the Duma but they rapidly found themselves sharing power with a council of workers – a 'soviet' – in the capital. Soon, similar soviets were set up in other parts of the country. Thus the revolution which had failed in 1905 triumphed in March 1917. As the Russian historian Berdyaev wrote:

Soviet: today it refers to a council elected in districts of the U.S.S.R. – the Union of Soviet Socialist Republics.

In 1905 the army remained loyal to the tsar. In 1917 it either stood aside or supported the revolutionaries. Petrograd was largely manned by conscripts rather than older, more experienced soldiers.

Medvedev here uses the old Russian system of dating. For 'February' read 'March'.

One cannot even say that the February Revolution overthrew the monarchy in Russia; the monarchy fell by itself; no one defended it; it had no supporters.
(Quoted in R. Medvedev, *The October Revolution*, 1979)

Lenin agreed, but felt that revolutionary propaganda had also had an effect:

It is beyond all doubt that the spontaneity of the movement is proof that it is deeply rooted in the masses, that its roots are firm, and that it is inevitable.
(Quoted in R. Medvedev, *The October Revolution*)

Lenin returns to Russia

Lenin was now in a frenzy of impatience to return to Russia. On 9 April Lenin, with 32 other passengers, left Zurich, bound for Russia. On the evening of 16 April he arrived at the Finland Station in Petrograd to be greeted rapturously by his supporters, with a speech of welcome from Chkeizdze, the Menshevik Chairman of the Petrograd Soviet. A Russian source describes the return:

The absence of the leader of the Party, Lenin, was felt. On April 3 [16] 1917, after a long period of exile, Lenin returned to Russia.

Copyright   **H.I.M. THE TSAR OF RUSSIA.** Stanley's Press Agency. Levitsky.

BELGIAN RELIEF FUNDS
1915
OFFICIAL SOUVENIR

Tsar Nicholas II, a cousin of George V.
The postcard is from a charity series.

Lenin's arrival was of tremendous importance to the Party and the workers, soldiers and sailors assembled at the Finland Railway Station and in the station square to welcome him. Their enthusiasm as Lenin alighted from the train was indescribable. They lifted their leader shoulder high and carried him to the main waiting room of the station. There the Mensheviks Chkeizdze and Skobelev launched into speeches of 'welcome' on behalf of the Petrograd Soviet, in which the 'expressed the hope' that they and Lenin would find a 'common language', But Lenin did not stop to listen; sweeping past them, he went out to the masses of workers and soldiers. Mounting an armoured car, he delivered his famous speech in which he called upon the masses to fight for the victory of the socialist revolution. 'Long live the socialist revolution!' were the words with which Lenin concluded this first speech after long years of exile.

(Anon, *The History of the Communist Party of the Soviet Union*, 1943)

What impression does this account seek to convey?

More detailed Soviet histories explain that the Bolsheviks had made an agreement with the German Ambassador in Switzerland:

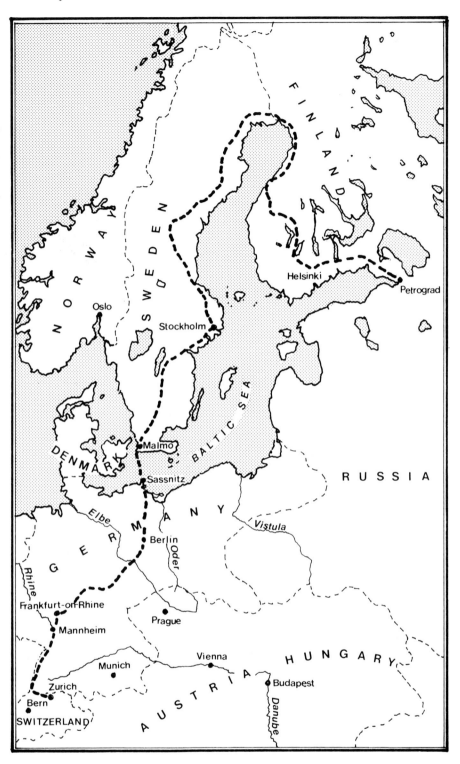

The route taken by Lenin back to Russia in April 1917.

Emigré: a person who decides to live abroad, usually for political reasons.

Extra-territorial: means belonging to no one country. Why was this an essential requirement for Lenin?

First, that all the emigrés should go, irrespective of their attitude towards the war; second, that the train in which they were to travel was to be an extra-territorial one; finally, that all passengers should agitate in Russia for the subsequent exchange of an equal number of Austro-German prisoners interned in Russia.
(Quoted in D. Shub, *Lenin: A Biography*, 1948)

However, two pieces of evidence from German sources tell us why the Germans were keen and willing to allow Lenin to return to Russia:

(a) Our government, in sending Lenin to Russia, took upon itself a tremendous responsibility. From a military point of view his journey was justified, for it was imperative that Russia should fall.
(General Ludendorff, *My War Reminiscences*, 1919)

Ludendorff was the German Chief of Staff.

(b) We naturally tried, by means of propaganda, to increase the disintegration that the Russian Revolution had introduced into the Army. Some man at home who had connections with the Russian revolutionaries exiled in Switzerland came upon the idea of employing some of them in order to hasten the undermining and poisoning of the moral of the Russian Army.

Mathias Erzberger was deputy at the Reichstag, the German parliament.

He applied to Erzberger and the deputy head of the German Foreign Office. And thus it came about that Lenin was conveyed through Germany to Petrograd in the manner that afterwards transpired.

In the same way as I send shells into the enemy trenches, as I discharge poison gas at him, I, as an enemy, have the right to employ the expedient of propaganda against his garrisons.
(General Hoffmann, *The War of Missed Opportunities*, 1924)

What were the German generals seeking to do? Why did Ludendorff nevertheless believe it was a 'tremendous responsibility'?

As the train prepared to depart for Russia, the following scene ensued:

Lenin's supporters milled around the waiting train carrying revolutionary banners and singing the 'Internationale'; his enemies, a group of anti-German Socialists, shouted, 'Spies! German spies! Look how happy they are – going home at the Kaiser's expense!'

Internationale: a revolutionary song adopted by socialists worldwide.

William II was the Kaiser, or emperor, of Germany.

Lenin stood at the window of his compartment, supporting his chin on the ledge, and shaking his head with a smile. As the demonstration continued, he started to get off the train, but one of his comrades held him back. The angry demonstrators seemed anxious to use their fists. Lenin returned to the car window. His followers on the platform again struck up the 'Internationale' to drown out the catcalls of their opponents. When the train pulled out, police were breaking up the fighting between the two groups.
(D. Shub, *Lenin: A Biography*)

Why was one group so opposed to Lenin's return to Russia?

Lenin had gained permission from the authorities to travel through Germany on his return to Russia, and it is also known that he accepted German cash.

Lenin's wife later wrote:

Of course, in giving us permission to travel, the German government was under the impression that revolution was a terrible disaster for a country and thought that, by allowing emigré internationalists through to their native country, they would help spread the 'disaster' in Russia. The Bolsheviks were very little concerned with what the bourgeois German government thought.
(Quoted in J.K. Galbraith's 'Lenin and the Great Ungluing', *The Listener*, 10 February 1977)

Internationalist: a supporter of the International – one of the associations formed to promote socialist or Communist action.

The American historian Adam Ulam writes:

Granted Lenin's premises, his decision to accept German help was perfectly natural. It was not to affect his position an iota: he was working to bring about a new revolution in Russia, but that revolution in turn was to overthrow the German government and bring about the victory of revolutionary socialism in all Europe. The Bolsheviks needed money. Their future prodigious growth in membership and prestige between April and October was to reflect not only the skill of their leaders and the ineptitude of their opponents, but also their superior resources.
(A. Ulam, *Lenin and the Bolsheviks*)

Why did Lenin need money? Do you think it mattered that it came from Germany?

Lenin nonetheless appreciated that travelling to Russia with the help of the Germans – with whom, after all, his country was still at war – would provide his opponents with a weapon to use against him. Unscrupulously he turned to a political enemy for help:

> Would the Petrograd Soviet and its chairman Menshevik Chkeizdze authorize the Bolsheviks' trips so as to prevent future slanders? Needless to say they were willing: it would have been undemocratic to prevent the arrival of the man who was coming with the announced intention of destroying them.
> (A. Ulam, *Lenin and the Bolsheviks*)

Do you think that Chkeizdze was foolish to welcome Lenin, or had he no other alternative? Can you detect any irony in Ulam's comments on Chkeizdze's decision?

Loyal Opposition or Insurrectionary Party?

Bolsheviks and Mensheviks

Lenin, even while still in Switzerland, reacted quickly to events in Russia during March 1917. In one of his 'Letters from Afar' Lenin addressed the Russian people:

> You performed miracles of proletarian heroism yesterday in overthrowing the tsarist monarchy. In the more or less near future . . . you will again have to perform the same miracles of heroism to overthrow the rule of the landlords and the capitalists . . . .
> (Quoted in Anon, *Lenin: A Short Biography*)

The Bolsheviks were urged to spread propaganda, keep apart from the other parties and work to bring the war to an end. Official Soviet sources blame Kamenev, a recently returned Bolshevik, for moderating and cutting Lenin's letters in *Pravda*. According to Alexander Shlyapikov Kamenev said:

If you had been a Bolshevik in Russia at this time, whose advice would you have followed, and why?

> It would be the most stupid policy when an army faces the enemy, to urge it to lay down arms and to go home. That would be a policy not of peace but of serfdom, a policy contemptuously rejected by the free nation.
> (Quoted in A. Ulam, *Lenin and the Bolsheviks*)

Kamenev was not alone in thinking this. In the interval between the tsar's fall and Lenin's return to Russia, Stalin came to Petrograd from exile in Siberia and took over control of *Pravda*. He held the moderate view that the Bolsheviks should link with the left wing of the Mensheviks, accept the benefits of the new freedom, and continue the war against Germany until a just peace could be obtained.

Pravda, the Communist Party newspaper, is published daily in the Soviet Union. On the left can be seen the date of the first publication.

The day after he returned to Petrograd Lenin presented *his* views to the

Bolsheviks in what have become known as the 'April Theses'. Trotsky summarized their main arguments:

The theses expressed simple thoughts in simple words comprehensible to all. The republic which has issued from the February revolution is not our republic, and the war which it is now raging is not our war. The task of the Bolsheviks is to overthrow the imperialist government . . . . We are in the minority. In these circumstances there can be no talk of violence from our side . . . . 'We must patiently explain.'
(L. Trotsky, *The History of the Russian Revolution*, Vol. I, 1932/3)

Lenin's ideas were rejected overwhelmingly by the Petrograd Bolshevik Committee. Shub describes their reaction:

His vehemence caused a storm of protest. There were catcalls and hisses while Lenin spoke. Alexander Bogdanov, his former close associate, interrupted Lenin by crying out: 'That is the delusion of a lunatic.'
(D. Shub, *Lenin: A Biography*)

Another Bolshevik, Sukhanov, believed that:

Lenin in his present state is so unacceptable to everybody that he represents absolutely no danger.
(Quoted in D. Shub, *Lenin: A Biography*)

The 'April Theses' were published in *Pravda*, and a few days later an editor in the same paper commented that:

The extreme reaction to Lenin's view was because it was widely believed that the February Revolution had overthrown the tsar and ushered in a period of bourgeois government, and that in the foreseeable future the soviets should support the Provisional Government. Hence the comment that Lenin's words were like an exploding bomb.
(Quoted in Anon, *Lenin: A Short Biography*)

Soviet sources suggest that:

The Party took Lenin's lead – approved his plan of struggle for the socialist revolution and made it the basis for its practical activities.
(Quoted in Anon, *Lenin: A Short Biography*)

It is part of Lenin's greatness that the Party eventually followed his lead, and that in time the Bolsheviks came to dominate the soviets. At first, however, his views were regarded as impractical.

The July Days

The Provisional Government believed it was necessary to continue the war in order to defeat Germany and keep the support and goodwill of fellow democracies Britain and France. On 4 May Lenin attacked, in *Pravda*, Foreign Minister Miliukov's determination to honour Russia's treaty obligations:

. . . . The alliance with the English and the French bankers has been declared sacred . . . . *Who* has concluded this alliance with '*our*' allies, i.e. with the Anglo-French billionaires? The tsar, Rasputin, the tsar's gang, of course. To Miliukov and Co., however, the treaty is sacred. . . . Die, tens of thousands of you everyday – because 'we' have not yet fought the thing to a finish, because we have not yet received our share of the loot! . . . The Provisional Government, the government of a handful of capitalists, must give way to the soviets.
(Quoted in J.S. Curtiss, *The Russian Revolutions of 1917*, 1957)

Why do you think fellow Bolsheviks reacted in this way? Would the Provisional Government have been pleased?

Rasputin was a holy-man with undue influence over the Russian royal family – particularly the tsarina. See p. 62.

What was Lenin linking the Provisional Government with? Why does he believe that Russia should have no part in the war?

Fraternization: when soldiers make friends with enemy troops.

Fraternization was beginning to take place at the Front and was to increase as the year progressed. *Izvestia* saw the danger from both Lenin's and the Germans' attempts to foster fraternization and on 15 May the paper appealed to the front-line troops:

Having sworn to protect Russian liberty, do not refuse to take the offensive if the war situation should demand it. The freedom and happiness of Russia are in your hands. . . . Those who tell you that fraternization is the way to peace, are leading both you and Russian freedom to destruction.
(Quoted in J.S. Curtiss, *The Russian Revolutions of 1917*)

How can you tell that this view is that of the Petrograd Soviet?

The Provisional Government continued to put the winning of the war as its first priority and in July an offensive was launched under General Brusilov. After initial successes the Germans began to counter-attack. A telegram from the South-Western Front of the 11th Army of the Minister of War described how:

July -20

Verst: a measure equal to 1067 kms.

For a distance of several hundred versts long files of deserters, both armed and unarmed, men who are in good health and robust, who have lost all shame and feel that they can act together with impunity, are proceeding to the rear of the army. Frequently entire units desert in this manner.
(Quoted in R.P. Browder and A.F. Kerensky, *The Russian Provisional Government, 1917*, 1961)

Why is this a useful source?

Bolshevik propaganda played a part in the disintegration of the Russian army. To the soldiers the Bolsheviks directed their slogan of 'Peace, Bread and Land', and to the peasants in the countryside and the workers in the towns such ideas were also attractive.

Bolshevik propaganda influenced events in Petrograd in July, when news of the German advance and the reluctance of Russian troops to go to the Front sparked off a series of actions which were to force Lenin into hiding in Finland. Trotsky summarized *Izvestia's* description of the events of July 16:

At five o'clock in the afternoon there came out, armed, the 1st Machine Gun, a part of the Moscow, and part of the Grenadier, and a part of the Pavlovsky Regiments. They were joined by crowds of workers . . . . By eight o'clock in the evening, separate parts of regiments began to pour towards the Palace of Kshesinskaia, armed to the teeth and with red banners and placards demanding the transfer of power to the Soviets. Speeches were made from the balcony. At ten-thirty a meeting was held on the square in front of the Tauride Palace . . . .
(L. Trotsky, *The History of the Russian Revolution*, Vol. II, 1932/3)

How does this extract illustrate the spread of Bolshevik propaganda?

The Soviet housed in the Tauride Palace argued hard and long with the demonstrators, and refused to take power.

The following day *Izvestia* carried a leading article entitled 'The Dangers of Revolution'. It concluded:

. . . we call upon the workers and soldiers of Petrograd to save the revolution, to save it not by reckless demonstrations which have already caused bloodshed of fraternal workers and soldiers, but by conscious, revolutionary discipline, by the subjection of their own will to the will of the majority. The revolution is in danger!
(Quoted in R.P. Browder and A.F. Kerensky, *The Russian Provisional Government, 1917*)

Which revolution was *Izvestia* referring to?

The Provisional Government: the government formed after the 'March Revolution'.

The Provisional Government had been preparing evidence of German links with the Bolsheviks. They could cite the sealed train, Bolshevik propaganda at the Front, and demonstrations in Petrograd. News of this was unofficially leaked and soon the tide began to turn against the

The July Days. Where might the photograph have been taken from, and what does it tell us?

Bolsheviks. Lenin realized that this was not the time for a successful uprising. Blood had already been spilt in Petrograd and lives lost, but now the Bolshevik Central Committee sought peaceful action:

Comrades! On Monday you came out on the streets. On Tuesday you decided to continue the demonstration. We called you to a peaceful demonstration yesterday. The object of this demonstration was to show to all the toiling and exploited masses the strength of our slogans, their weight, their significance.
  Comrades! For the present political crisis, our aim has been accomplished. We have therefore decided to end this demonstration. Let each and every one peacefully and in an organized manner bring the strike and the demonstration to a close.
(Quoted in R.P. Browder and A.F. Kerensky, *The Russian Provisional Government, 1917*)

What was the purpose of the Bolshevik declaration?

By 20 July order had been restored and warrants issued for the arrest of the leading Bolsheviks. The Provisional Government started a campaign of slander against Lenin and his supporters in an attempt to render the Bolshevik Party leaderless. It outlawed Lenin, issued a warrant for his arrest and took all steps to seize or assassinate him. Lenin was fortunate to escape. The offices of *Pravda* were raided only half an hour after he had left them.
  Lenin was not to return to Russia until the eve of the October Revolution. Of Lenin's chief associates, Trotsky and Kamenev were arrested, Zinoviev disappeared, and only Stalin evaded capture. The Bolsheviks now faced a

July Days: the name given to the premature Bolshevik uprising.

Do you think that Trotsky was being wise after the event, or would he have held this view at the time?

real setback and were forced underground. Writing in exile in the 1930s, Trotsky commented on the July Days:

> But nevertheless the leadership of the party was completely right in not taking the road of armed insurrection. It is not enough to seize power – you have to hold it.
> (L. Trotsky, *History of the Russian Revolution*, Vol. II)

Bolshevik Coup d'Etat or Bolshevik Revolution?

'All power to the Bolsheviks!'

From the very moment when the tsar abdicated in March 1917 the Provisional Government had only a tenuous hold on the reins of power. The Duma moderates who led it had had no previous experience of government and, moreover, they had to share political authority with the Petrograd Soviet. Although the Bolsheviks were suppressed in July the Provisional Government became increasingly weaker as its political priorities became more and more out of touch with the wishes of the mass of the people. The war continued yet Russia was weary. The Provisional Government only moved slowly in distributing the nobles' land among the peasants, yet the mood of the peasants was clearly demonstrated in the many cases of forcible seizures of land. The Bolsheviks offered peace (they alone of all parties had opposed the war since its outbreak) and from mid-1917, they advocated the immediate dispersal of landed estates amongst the peasants.

Was this not cynical for a party opposed to the possession of private property?

In his Finnish hiding-place Lenin wrote a pamphlet entitled *State and Revolution* in which he argued that a socialist state would not emerge out of a bourgeois one (such as the Provisional Government represented). This could only be achieved by a revolutionary proletariat which would oppose capitalism with force. Lenin also stressed the need for a worker-peasant alliance.

Where had Lenin learnt this lesson?

The failure of the Brusilov Offensive had seen the fall of the government led by Prince Lvov, and on 21 July he was replaced by Kerensky, a Socialist Revolutionary, a member of the Soviet and a former Minister of Justice. Brusilov had already been replaced by the Cossack general, Kornilov as Commander-in-Chief of the Army. Many conservatives felt that the Provisional Government was not conducting the war as well as it should, and that the suspension of the death penalty had led to a loss of discipline in the army ranks.

Divisions were appearing within the Provisional Government. Kerensky organized a huge conference in Moscow on 7 August in an attempt to unite the Russian people. When Kornilov rose to speak, the right-wingers gave him a noisy ovation, but the soldiers sat still. Shouts of 'Stand up, soldiers' were met with no response. The divisions were there for all to see.

After the conference Kornilov, with the support of many army officers, landowners and industrialists, tried to take control of the Provisional Government. Kerensky had hoped to use him to settle his old scores with the Bolsheviks, but Kornilov felt that the time had come for a dictatorship. Therefore on 9 September Kerensky ordered Kornilov's dismissal and summoned him to Petrograd. Kornilov refused and the following day issued a proclamation to the Russian people:

> People of Russia, our great country is dying. Her end is near. Forced to speak openly, I, General Kornilov, declare that the Provisional Government, under the

*The cover of a pamphlet reprinting one of
Lenin's speeches from 1917. What
impression does it seek to convey?*

Why did Kornilov use the name of the
Bolsheviks to argue his case?

pressure of the Bolshevik majority in the Soviet, is acting in complete harmony
with the German General staff and . . . is killing the army and shaking the country.
(Quoted in J.S. Curtiss, *The Russian Revolutions of 1917*)

The revolt led by Kornilov failed because the Petrograd Soviet and many
of the troops still supported the Provisional Government. A general strike
was called, but the railway workers refused to allow the trains carrying
troops loyal to Kornilov to enter Petrograd, and the revolt was put down.

Kerensky and the Provisional Government survived, but how did
Kornilov's revolt reveal their weaknesses? Remember that Kerensky was
committed to winning the war to ensure the success of the revolution. Read
the following extracts, then come to your decision:

(a)   *A military intelligence report*

In their conversations with the soldiers, the officer personnel, acting in the interests of combat duty, always tried to raise in the eyes of the soldiers the prestige of General Kornilov . . . now, when the Government has accused General Kornilov of treason, . . . all the officers who had spoken well of Kornilov have become in the eyes of the soldiers counter-revolutionaries who should be arrested.

(b)   *A newspaper editorial*

Don't the leaders of the democracy really understand, or are they unwilling to understand that further tolerance is impossible; that the policy of compromises and agreements with Bolshevism has already disintegrated Russia, and will eventually ruin the revolution, the country, and democracy itself.

In Tashkent, the soldiers, egged on by Bolshevism, stage a revolt which the Provisional Government is putting down with machine guns. Through its outrages Bolshevism not only caused a revolt in Tashkent, but is encouraging the seceding of the entire oblast . . . .

(Quoted in R.P. Browder and A.F. Kerensky, *The Russian Provisional Government, 1917*)

> **Tashkent, a town in Central Asia, was taken by Russian forces in 1865. Today it is the capital of Uzbekistan.**
>
> **Oblast**: district, in Russia.

Kerenksy's position continued to worsen and his last card was the calling of a constituent assembly, elections for which were announced for 8 December. Meanwhile he made a number of concessions, allowing several Bolsheviks to be released from prison because the Bolsheviks as a whole had helped crush Kornilov's revolt.

While the country foundered, the Bolsheviks maintained their drive and organization, and in elections to the city soviets in September they gained 50 per cent of the seats, compared with 10 per cent in July. The Bolsheviks also improved their position in the soldiers' soviets. One of those released from jail was Trotsky, who was soon elected President of the Petrograd Soviet, supported by the Bolsheviks and the left wing of the Socialist Revolutionary Party.

As soon as the Bolsheviks gained control of the soviets in Moscow and Petrograd, Lenin moved onto the offensive. The danger now lay, not in acting too soon, but in lagging. The slogan 'All Power to the Soviets', dropped by Lenin after the July Days, was re-introduced, because it now meant 'All power to the Bolsheviks'.

> **Why did the slogan change in meaning?**

In the middle of September Lenin appeared secretly in Petrograd, to attend the Central Committee meeting of the Bolshevik Party. He spoke strongly in favour of an uprising:

Lenin states that since the beginning of September a certain indifference towards the question of uprising has been noted. He says that it is inadmissible if we earnestly raise the slogan of seizure of power by the Soviets. It is, therefore, high time to turn attention to the technical side of the question. Much time has obviously been lost.

(Quoted in R.P. Browder and A.F. Kerensky, *The Russian Provisional Government, 1917*)

Two members of the Central Committee, Zinoviev and Kamenev, opposed Lenin's views. They argued that the failure of the July rising had been a severe setback to the Bolsheviks. Why risk another failure when they could gain power peacefully in the elections?

> **How would you have voted on this question?**

However, Lenin's argument won the day, with ten votes for and only two against. Trotsky has been criticized for his views on the matter:

Trotsky did not come out openly against the resolution of the C.C. [Central Committee] on the armed uprising, but insisted on having it put off until the convocation of the Second Congress of Soviets, which was tantamount to obstructing the rising. Lenin strongly opposed this position. . . . . 'To wait for the Congress of Soviets would be utter idiocy, or sheer treachery,' he wrote.

(Anon, *Lenin: A Short Biography*)

> **Why do you think that Trotsky advised delay?**

Ten days that shook the world

The division within the Bolshevik Central Committee, and of the plan for an armed uprising, became public news following an article in *Novaya Zhizn* written by Zinoviev and Kamenev.

However, events were playing into the hands of the Bolsheviks. Rumours spread that the capital was to be transferred from Petrograd to Moscow, because of the fear of a German invasion. This led the Petrograd Soviet to form a Military Revolutionary Committee to supervise troop movements. Trotsky was elected Chairman and thus the Bolsheviks gained virtual control of the Petrograd garrison.

Fait accompli: a thing done and no longer worth arguing about.

The All Russian Congress of Soviets was due to meet on 2 November but was delayed for five days. The Bolsheviks, hoping to present the Congress with a *fait accompli*, decided that this would be the day of the uprising. In an attempted pre-emptive strike on 6 November, Kerensky tried to take action against the Bolsheviks before they were fully prepared. The Bolshevik newspaper *Rabochi Put* ('The Path of Labour') was closed down. This was the spark for action.

The first Congress met in Petrograd in June 1917, with representatives from more than 350 units from all over Russia. It appointed a Central Executive Committee which sat permanently between Congress meetings.

The American journalist John Reed was an eyewitness of these events. He later wrote:

This was the Bolshevik headquarters, located in a private school on the outskirts of Petrograd.

> Towards four in the morning [of 7 November] I met Zorin in the outer hall of the Smolny Institute, a rifle slung from his shoulder.
> 'We're moving,' said he, calmly, but with satisfaction. 'We pinched the Assistant Minister of Justice and the Minister of Religions. They're down in the cellar now. Our regiment is on the march to capture the Telephone Exchange, another the Telegraph Agency, another the State Bank. The Red Guard is out . . . .'

Why did the revolutionaries first seize the Telephone Exchange, the Telegraph Agency and the State Bank?

> Far over the still roofs westwards came the sound of scattered rifle fire . . . .

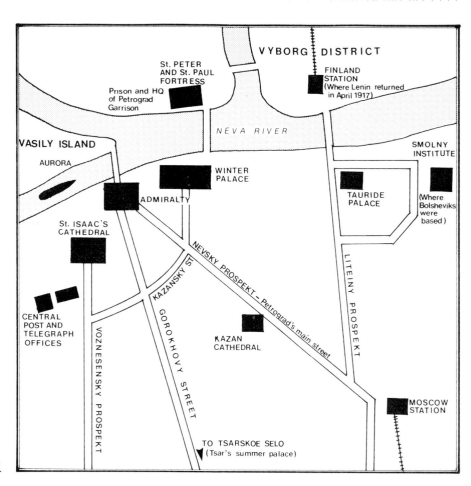

Petrograd in 1917.

Behind us, great Smolny, bright with lights, hummed like a gigantic hive . . . .
(J. Reed, *Ten Days that Shook the World*, 1926)

The Winter Palace was the Petrograd home of the Tsar and his family. It now houses the famous Hermitage Museum.

The Winter Palace, where the Provisional Government was meeting, was surrounded.

Petrograd on 7 November
Petrograd looked as usual during the course of the day. Street-cars ran almost as usual. Here and there routes were changed, owing to the opening of the Nikolaevsky Bridge to let warships pass. As usual they were overcrowded . . . [Soldiers] from every part of the garrison are on guard and on picket duty . . . to preserve order . . . . The Military Revolutionary Committee . . . has also issued appeals to the people [to keep order] . . . .
(Quoted in J. Bunyan and H.H. Fisher, *The Bolshevik Revolution, 1917-1918*)

What does this extract tell us about the success of Bolshevik planning? It is taken from *Delo Naroda* ('People's Deed'), a Socialist Revolutionary paper hostile to the Bolsheviks. Is this likely to make the extract more or less, useful as evidence?

Little blood was shed. The crucial takeover of power in Petrograd was effected with almost nonchalant ease, and the lack of popular support for the Provisional Government was cruelly exposed.

The 'revolution' reached its climax in the much-publicized, much-filmed, but largely fabricated, 'Storming of the Winter Palace'. S.L. Maslov, the Minister for Agriculture, described what happened in *Delo Naroda*, 11 November:

'The Storming of the Winter Palace' by N. Kochergin. Compare the detail of this painting with other information given in the text.

The guard of the Winter Palace was made up of some cadets, part of the Engineering School, two companies of Cossacks, and a small number of the Women's Battalion.

At 10.00 [p.m.] a shot was fired in the palace, followed by cries and shots from the cadets. On investigation it appeared that two sailors had climbed to the upper

storey of the palace and had thrown down two hand grenades. The bombs wounded two cadets . . .

The sailors were arrested and disarmed. A search was made throughout the building and about fifty hostile sailors and soldiers were arrested and disarmed. In the meantime more and more . . . arrived until the guard seemed helpless. Outside the palace, rifles, machine-guns, and even cannon were being fired. About two in the morning there was a loud noise at the entrance to the palace . . . . The armed mob of soldiers, sailors, and civilians, led by Antonov, broke in. They shouted threats and made jokes. Antonov arrested everybody in the name of the Revolutionary Committee and proceeded to take the names of all present . . . . He inquired for Kerensky, but he was no longer in the palace.

(Quoted in J. Bunyan and H.H. Fisher, *The Bolshevik Revolution, 1917-1918*)

> Compare this statement with the painting of the storming of the Winter Palace. Which rings true?

Kerensky had left Petrograd in an effort to raise loyal troops, but he was not to return.

Modern Soviet sources describe the victory as follows:

The Bolshevik Party, headed by Lenin, led the people of Russia to their great victory. The victory of October [November] was the triumph of Leninism, a result of the hard painstaking work, the heroic intense struggle, which the Bolshevik Leninists carried on in the course of many years. . . . It was a true revolution of the people.

(Anon, *Lenin: A Short Biography*)

> Lenin had clearly played an enormous part in the events of 1917. Look back and list what you consider to be the most important. To what do you attribute his success?

Western historians often take a cooler view of these events. It is hard to see the Bolshevik coup as a seizure of power since the Provisional Government was so weak by November 1917 that it could hardly offer any resistance. It has been estimated that no more than five thousand people, on both sides,

> *'Lenin Speaking at the Second All Russian Congress of Soviets' by V. Serov. What group forms a large part of the audience?*

took part in this 'revolution'. In fact the 'revolution' was a limited conflict between two quite small groups. The vast majority of Russians were completely uninvolved at this stage. As one writer has aptly put it, 'the Bolsheviks had not captured a Ship of State, they had boarded a derelict.'

Meanwhile, the second All Russian Congress of Soviets met on the same evening that the Winter Palace was being attacked. In protest, the Socialist Revolutionaries and the Mensheviks walked out, leaving the Bolsheviks in complete control. Trotsky was triumphant: 'Your role is played out, go where you belong from now on – into the dustbin of history'.

On the evening of 7 November John Reed read the following proclamation in a Bolshevik paper:

> TO THE CITIZENS OF RUSSIA!
>
> The Provisional Government is deposed. The State Power has passed into the hands of the organ of the Petrograd Soviet of Workers' and Soldiers' Deputies, the Military Revolutionary Committee, which stands at the head of Petrograd Proletariat and garrison.
>
> The cause for which the people were fighting: immediate proposal of a democratic peace, abolition of landlord property-rights over the land, labour control over production, creation of a Soviet Government – that cause is securely achieved.
>
> LONG LIVE THE REVOLUTION OF WORKMEN, SOLDIERS, AND PEASANTS!
>
> *Military Revolutionary Committee*
> *Petrograd Soviet of Workers' and Soldiers' Deputies*
> (Quoted in J. Reed, *Ten Days that Shook the World*)

Why is this a clever piece of propaganda?

People's Democracy or Bolshevik Dictatorship?

'Long live the Revolution!'

The second revolution of 1917 had been organized by the Bolshevik party, on behalf of, and with the support of, many workers and soldiers in Petrograd. Their power was soon to be extended to Moscow and several other cities. In the countryside, meanwhile, many peasants still supported the peasants' party, the Socialist Revolutionaries, but as Arthur Ransome, a British newspaper correspondent, wrote a month late: 'The soviets at least have real authority'.

Resistance was there, nonetheless, and was to eventually develop into civil war. With the suppression of all opposition parties except the left wing of the S.R.s – who continued to support the Bolsheviks – a decree was published on 9 November in *Izvestia*:

> TO ALL WORKERS, SOLDIERS, AND PEASANTS:
>
> . . . supported by an overwhelming majority of the workers, soldiers, and peasants, and basing itself on the victorious insurrection of the workers and the garrison of Petrograd, the Congress hereby resolves to take power into its own hands.
>
> The Provisional Government is deposed and most of its members are under arrest.
>
> The Soviet authority will at once propose a democratic peace to all nations and an immediate armistice on all fronts. It will safeguard the transfer without compensation of all land . . . to the peasant committees; it will defend soldiers' rights, . . . it will establish workers' control over industry, it will insure the convocation of the Constituent Assembly on the date set, it will supply the cities with bread and the villages with articles of first necessity, and it will secure to all nationalities inhabiting Russia the right of self-determination. . . . Soldiers! Resist

'Congress' here refers to the Congress of Soviets.

Kerensky; who is a Kornilovist! Be on guard! Railwaymen! Stop all echelons [groups] sent by Kerensky against Petrograd! Soldiers, Workers, Employees! The fate of the Revolution and democratic peace is in your hands!

LONG LIVE THE REVOLUTION!

The All-Russian Congress of Soviets of Workers' and Soldiers' Deputies.
Delegates from the Peasants' Soviets.
(Quoted in J. Bunyan and H.H. Fisher, *The Bolshevik Revolution, 1917-1918*)

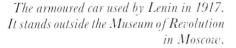

How did the Bolsheviks seek to allay fears and satisfy grievances? Do you consider this an effective statement?

Next the All Russian Congress of Soviets was presented with the following plan for their approval:

By decree of the All Russian Congress of Soviets a Provisional Workers' and Peasants' Government, to be known as the Soviet of People's Commissars, is formed to govern the country until the meeting of the Constituent Assembly.
(Quoted in J. Bunyan and H.H. Fisher, *The Bolshevik Revolution, 1917-1918*)

Lenin was named President of the Soviet; Trotsky, Commissar for Foreign Affairs; and Stalin, Chairman for Nationalities.

Trotsky later recalled how the name 'Commissar' was chosen:

'What name shall we use?' Lenin considered aloud.
'Not minister, that is a repulsive, worn-out designation.'
'We might say commissars', I suggested, 'but there are too many commissars now. Perhaps Chief Commissar . . . .'
'No, "chief" sounds bad. What about people's commissars?' . . . .
'People's Commissars? As for me, I like it. And the government as a whole?'
'Council of People's Commissars?' 'Council of People's Commissars', Lenin repeated. 'That is splendid. That smells of revolution.'
(Quoted in J. Bunyan and H.H. Fisher, *The Bolshevik Revolution, 1917-1918*)

The armoured car used by Lenin in 1917. It stands outside the Museum of Revolution in Moscow.

Events had certainly moved at a furious pace. In his autobiography, *My Life* (1930), Trotsky recounted a conversation with Lenin on the first evening after the victory:

Why would Lenin speak in German?

Lenin's wide-awake eyes rested on my tired face. 'You know,' he said hesitatingly, 'to pass so suddenly from persecution and underground living to a position of power . . .'. He searched for words and then suddenly finished in German – 'it makes one dizzy' – and moved his hand around his head. We looked at one another and smiled.
(Quoted in G. von Rauch, *A History of Soviet Russia*)

Retaining power

The Bolsheviks' problems were only beginning. Lenin had to deal with two parallel problems. Firstly that of retaining power in the face of an opposition which ranged from revolutionary groups which felt that Lenin had hijacked the Revolution, to ex-tsarists or those who simply wanted a return to the old order. The second problem was preventing the country from descending further into chaos and anarchy.

Many of the Bolshevik slogans had served their purpose and weakened the Provisional Government, but now the army was a shambles, and the countryside in chaos, with the peasants seizing the land, not for the state, but for themselves. Many observers felt that the inexperienced Bolsheviks would be unable to cope; that they were untried amateurs, without the experience necessary to govern the country. Moreover the only revolutionary precedent that the Bolsheviks themselves were prepared to recognize – the Paris Commune of 1871 – pointed to a disappointing lesson: the rest of France had refused to follow the revolutionary example of Paris, thus condemning the Commune to certain defeat. The historical parallel between Paris in 1871 and Petrograd in 1917 seemed clear and gave no cause for Bolshevik optimism. However, the critics and the doubters were soon to be proved wrong.

The Paris Commune was the name given to the revolutionary government which seized power in the French capital after the Franco-Prussian War.

Lenin swiftly introduced various decrees. He called for peace and an end to Russia's involvement in the First World War. Private ownership of land was ended; all was henceforth to belong to the state. Social ranks were abolished, freedom of religion granted, and foreign loans repudiated (the Bolsheviks simply refused to repay them). These actions alone would not have retained power for the Bolsheviks, however, and Lenin realized that force would be necessary. Ruthless action was taken, therefore, against all enemies of the new Bolshevik state.

To this end, Lenin created on 20 December the Cheka (now known as the K.G.B.), a political police force. One of its founders, Latsis, described its purpose. Its first task was:

To cut off at the roots all counter-revolution and sabotage in Russia; to hand over to the revolutionary court all those who are guilty of such attempts; to work out measures for dealing with such cases; and to enforce these measures without mercy . . . . It was necessary to make the foe feel that there was everywhere about him a seeing eye and a heavy hand ready to come down on him the moment he undertook anything against the Soviet government .`. . . .

Why did Latsis believe it was necessary to act quickly against the opposition?

(Quoted in J. Bunyan and H.H. Fisher, *The Bolshevik Revolution, 1917-1918*)

Later, in a conversation with Maxim Gorky, Lenin remarked:

The cruelty of our life, which is forced upon us by circumstances, will one day be understood and condoned.
(Quoted in L. Schapiro and P. Reddaway (eds), *Lenin*, 1967)

Dzerzhinsky was of Polish noble descent. A square in the centre of Moscow is named after him.

Dzerzhinsky, leader of the fledgling Cheka, announced in his first speech:

> Do not believe that I am concerned with formal justice. We do not need any laws now. What we need is to fight to the end. I request, I demand, the forging of the revolutionary sword that will annihilate all counter-revolutionaries!

(Quoted in G. von Rauch, *A History of Soviet Russia*)

Action was taken against all those opposed to the new régime. These included not only well born ex-tsarists, but also workers and peasants.

Arthur Ransome sent the following tribute to Dzerzhinsky to his newspaper in the Autumn of 1918:

Dzerzhinsky is seen today as a revolutionary hero in the Soviet Union. Opponents see him as a ruthless leader. How can people reach such different conclusions?

> He is a calm, cool-headed fanatic for the revolution with absolute trust in his own conscience and recognizing no higher court . . . . He has a theory of self-sacrifice in which one man has to take on himself the unpleasantness that would otherwise be shared by many. Hence his willingness to occupy his present position.

(Quoted in H. Brogan, *The Life of Arthur Ransome*, 1984)

Execution, confessions extracted by torture and threats became the order of the day. Clearly the Cheka, under the efficient and ruthless leadership of Dzerzhinsky, played a part in the Bolsheviks' retention of power – but at enormous social cost.

The postponement of elections for the Constituent Assembly had been one of the causes of Kerensky's downfall. Thus on 25 November elections finally took place. The results were as follows:

Left Socialist Revolutionaries: those on the extreme – the peasants' party.

Narodniki: peasant socialists.

Cadets: the party of the middle classes. Founded in 1905 they sought a constitutional government brought about by peaceful means. The party was suppressed in 1917.

National Minorities: the Russian Empire contained a large number of non-Russian people, as does the USSR today. They included Uzbeks, Ukrainians, Armenians and Georgians.

Socialist Revolutionaries	370
Bolsheviks	175
Left Socialist Revolutionaries	40
Mensheviks	16
Narodniki	2
Cadets	17
National minorities	86
Independent	1
	707

Roughly 50 per cent of the electorate had voted and the Bolsheviks were in the minority, as Lenin had anticipated. However, they gained the majority of seats in Moscow and Petrograd. The Assembly was due to open in December, but was delayed until January. During this time delegates arrived in Petrograd from all over Russia and an intense propaganda campaign took place. The S.R.s argued 'All Power to the Constituent Assembly' while the Bolsheviks used their real power to ban the Cadet party, and on certain occasions forcefully break up peaceful demonstrations.

Finally, on 18 January, the Constituent Assembly met for the first time, at the Tauride Palace. The doors were manned by Red Guards and heavily armed sailors. Some delegates, fearing that the Bolsheviks would cut off the lights to prevent them meeting, brought candles. Trotsky commented, in *Lenin*:

> Thus democracy entered upon the struggle with dictatorship heavily armed with sandwiches and candles.

(Quoted in J. Bunyan and H.H. Fisher, *The Bolshevik Revolution, 1917-1918*)

Sovnarkom: the leading council within the Assembly, headed by Lenin.

The galleries were packed with Bolshevik supporters, who loudly heckled the other parties. As was expected, the S.R.s refused to accept the various decrees of the Sovnarkom which they were asked to 'rubber stamp'. The session closed in chaos. The next day the doors were closed, and again guarded by Red Guards and sailors. The Constituent Assembly had been suppressed.

Lenin had argued the case for the suppression of the Constituent Assembly before the Bolshevik Central Committee:

All power to the soviets we said then, and for this we are fighting. The people desired to call a Constituent Assembly, and we called it. But it [the people] soon realized what this vaunted Constituent Assembly really represents. And now, once more, we are fulfilling the will of the people, which declared: All power to the soviets! And we shall crush the saboteurs . . . . The Constituent Assembly, which failed to recognize the power of the people, is now dispersed by the will of the soviet power . . . . The Soviet Republic will triumph, no matter what happens.
(Quoted in J. Bunyan and H.H. Fisher, *The Bolshevik Revolution, 1917-1918*)

What did Lenin mean by 'the will of the Soviet power'? Why doesn't he refer to the Bolsheviks?

Maxim Gorky, writing in *Novaya Zhizn* on 22 January 1918, attacked the closure of the Assembly, and in particular the crushing of a peaceful demonstration on 18 January:

Just as on 22 January, 1905, so on 18 January, 1918, there are people who . . . ask those who fired: 'Idiots, what are you doing? These are your own brothers. Can't you see the red banners? There is not a single banner hostile to the working class, or to you!'

Now, just as then, the soldiers reply: 'We have orders to shoot . . .'.

I ask the 'People's Commissars', among whom there should be honest and sensible men, if they understand that in putting the halter on their necks they are crushing the Russian democracy, destroying the conquests of the Revolution?

Do they understand this? or do they think: 'Ourselves or no one, even if it leads to destruction?'
(Quoted in J. Bunyan and H.H. Fisher, *The Bolshevik Revolution, 1917-1918*)

What link does Gorky make between 1905 and 1918? Was the calling and subsequent suppression of the Constituent Assembly another example of Lenin's shrewdness and ruthlessness? Or was it, as Gorky argues, a case of 'power at any cost'?

The suppression of the Constituent Assembly marks the end of what many people regard as the most valuable period of the Revolution. The reforms of the Bolsheviks since the coup of November had created a sense of excitement and liberation in Russia. Now, the Bolsheviks, with their secret police and their defiance and dispersal of the democratically elected Constituent Assembly, showed themselves to be as ruthless as the tsars. In a very real sense January 1918 was the time when the Bolsheviks seized power; the events of November 1917 were a 'revolution' in name alone.

From Brest-Litovsk to the New Economic Policy

A separate peace

In 1918 few people felt that the inexperienced Bolsheviks would retain power. They held only the two main cities, Moscow and Petrograd, along with the central and northern provinces and a few towns in Siberia and Central Asia. At the end of 1917 there were no more than 250,000 Bolshevik party members. Ranged against them were four groups. First, there were the moderate Socialist Revolutionaries with whom the Bolsheviks had refused to share power. The S.R.s, many of whom had sided with the Bolsheviks at first, after the suppression of the Constituent Assembly now sought to re-establish it. Second, there were various non-Russian groups which had been brought under the tsar's rule in previous centuries; these now took advantage of the internal chaos in Russia to form their own independent republics. Third, there were the ex-tsarist officers and the politicians of the Provisional Government who were opposed not only to the Bolsheviks, but also to the break-up of the Russian Empire. These various groups had only one thing in common: a hatred of Lenin and the Bolsheviks.

In addition there were the Germans. Lenin knew that the war against Germany could not be continued; the army was in disarray and peace was necessary. Pleas to the Allies for an armistice fell upon deaf ears, but eventually truce negotiations with Germany and Austria-Hungary began at Brest-Litovsk on 3 December 1917. Three weeks later, peace talks began, with Trotsky as the chief negotiator. He sought to drag out negotiations in the hope that a revolution would occur in Germany. This would mean that the heavy German demands on Russian territory would not have to be met.

By February the Germans' patience was exhausted and they presented Trotsky with an ultimatum. Trotsky refused to sign the treaty, declaring that the war was at an end and a 'no peace, no war' situation existed. Thus on 18 February 1918 the Germans resumed their offensive, pushing through the Baltic States and threatening Russia's capital. Plans were made to transfer the seat of power to Moscow. The situation was dire. In the south the Germans backed an independent Ukraine which had also been recognized by Britain and France.

In the Sovnarkom an angry debate took place. Some Bolsheviks such as Bukharin believed that Russia should pursue a revolutionary war, and stand up to the enemy and resist, even if it meant defeat and destruction. Lenin took an entirely different view. He claimed to speak for the Russian peasant, and urged a peace settlement:

> We cannot joke with war . . . . The people will not understand what we are trying to do . . . . If we meant war, we had no right to demobilize . . . . The Revolution will surely crash if we pursue a half-way policy. To delay is to betray the Revolution . . . . History will condemn us . . . when we had the choice of signing a peace [treaty] . . . . This is no time to exchange notes . . . . It is too late to send out feelers . . . . The revolution in Germany has not begun, and we know that it takes time for a revolution to triumph.
> (Quoted in J. Bunyan and H.H. Fisher, *The Bolshevik Revolution, 1917-1918*)

Bukharin (1888-1938) was a leading Bolshevik theorist. Between 1917 and 1928 he edited *Pravda*, but in 1928 disagreed with Stalin over his policy for industry. He was shot in 1938, accused of crimes against the state. In 1988, after many years campaigning by his widow, he was officially declared blameless for the crimes for which he was executed.

How would you describe Lenin's arguments? How do they differ from those of Bukharin and Trotsky?

Lenin's view won the day by the narrowest of margins – seven votes to six, with Trotsky changing sides to give his support. Lenin's efforts to win over the opposition are one of his greatest achievements, because he realized that a breathing space was necessary before the civil war which would undoubtedly begin against the Communists' internal opponents.

The Treaty of Brest-Litovsk, signed on 3 March 1918, was a dictated peace settlement in which Russia lost 26 per cent of her population, 27 per cent of her cultivable area, 26 per cent of her railways and 75 per cent of her coal mines. Iron and steel production also suffered greatly. One of the direct consequences of the peace settlement was the dissolution of the Bolshevik's coalition with the left-wing S.R.s. At the Seventh Party Congress on 6 March 1918 the R.S.D.L.P. (the Bolsheviks) changed its name to the Communist Party. It was also decided that the capital should be moved to Moscow.

Russia was now alone. She had cancelled the loans borrowed from her allies and published the secret treaties which the tsarist government had made with them. She had no friends, and soon the Allies would be supporting the opponents of Lenin's government.

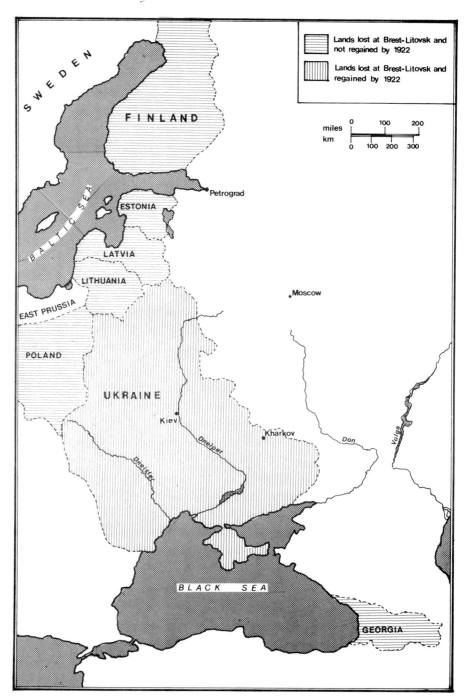

Territory lost by Russia between 1918 and 1920. Does the map suggest that Lenin was wise to concede territory at Brest-Litovsk?

Civil War

To begin with, the Allies – the Japanese and Americans in Siberia, the French in the south and the British in the north – intervened to defeat the Bolsheviks in order to bring Russia back into the war against Germany. But after Germany surrendered in November 1918 Allied intervention was designed to prevent the spread of Communism and to reclaim the companies and the property which the Bolsheviks had confiscated, and the loans which they failed to repay.

Meanwhile, in April 1918 Lenin wrote:

We the Bolshevik Party have convinced Russia. We have *won* Russia from the rich

for the poor, from the exploiters for the working people. Now we must administer Russia.
(Quoted in R. Medvedev, *The October Revolution*)

Little did Lenin know that his breathing space was to last only three months. In the meantime, as the Commissar for Education, A.V. Lunacharsky, wrote in 1921:

Everything was swept along in a turbulent current, flooded with revolutionary enthusiasm. It was necessary above all to give full voice to our ideals and ruthlessly crush whatever did not accord with them.
(Quoted in R. Medvedev, *The October Revolution*)

Lenin expressed similar thoughts:

We expected to accomplish economic tasks just as great as the political and military tasks we had accomplished by relying directly on this enthusiasm. We expected . . . to be able to organize the state production and the state distribution of products on Communist lines in a small peasant country.
(Quoted in R. Medvedev, *The October Revolution*)

<table>
<tr><td>Remember that this was the first communist state and thus they had no examples to follow.</td></tr>
</table>

The left-wing Bolsheviks wanted Communism straight away and urged that all private property should be placed in the hands of the state. Even Lenin in 1917 had said that 'all citizens should work equally, do their proper share of work, and get equal pay . . . . The whole of society will . . . become a single office and a single factory, with equality of labour and pay.' Later, however, in 1921, Lenin openly stated that everyone had sought to move too quickly.

One of Lenin's major problems was getting sufficient food to the towns which were the main centres of Bolshevik support. The Bolsheviks at first introduced a grain monopoly and established a fixed price for this foodstuff. The result was that the peasants, if they had any surplus at all, did not wish to sell it either for low prices or in exchange for poor quality goods. In order to increase supplies, armed workers' detachments were formed in the towns and sent into the countryside to requisition grain.

On 13 May 1918 the Sovnarkom published a decree introducing, in effect, a food dictatorship:

The peasant bourgeoisie, having accumulated in their cash boxes enormous sums of money, which they extorted from the state during the war, remain stubbornly indifferent to the groans of the starving workers and poor peasants; they will not bring their grain to the collection points, thinking to force the government to raise prices again, so that they can sell their grain at fabulous prices to grain speculators and 'bag traders'. The greedy stubbornness of the village Kulaks and rich peasants must be brought to an end . . . . Only one way out remains – to answer the violence of the grain owners against the starving poor with violence against the grain hoarders. Not one pood of grain should remain in the hands of the peasants beyond the amount required for the sowing of their fields and the feeding of their families until the next harvest.
(Quoted in J. Bunyan and H.H. Fisher, *The Bolshevik Revolution, 1917-1918*)

<table>
<tr><td>**Kulaks**: wealthier peasants, who often employed others. Encouraged by Stolypin and later persecuted by Stalin.

Pood: a Russian measure of weight equal to 16.38 kg.

How and why does Sovnarkom describe the violence of the grain owners?</td></tr>
</table>

Lenin took a great interest in the formation of these units. On 10 May 1918 he sent a worker, Ivanov, to the Commissariat of Food Supply with the following letter:

The bearer . . . is a Putilov factory worker . . . . I told him about yesterday's decree and the decision that the Commissariat of Labour was urgently to mobilize workers. I gave him my opinion as follows:

Waiting for the bread ration in 1918. The walls of the building behind show signs of the recent conflict.

Unless the best workers of Petrograd build by *selection* a reliable workers' army of 20,000 people for a disciplined and ruthless *military* crusade against the rural bourgeoisie and against bribe-takers, famine and the ruin of the Revolution are inevitable. Please confirm this to the bearer and give him a brief statement that you will grant such detachments the fullest powers . . . .
(Quoted in R. Medvedev, *The October Revolution*)

On another occasion he urged the amendment of the food decree:

What was likely to be the response of the peasants to these actions?

Lay it down more precisely that owners of grain who possess surplus grain and do not send it to the depots . . . will be declared enemies of the people and will be subject to imprisonment for a term of not less than ten years, confiscation of their property, and expulsion forever from the community.
(Quoted in R. Medvedev, *The October Revolution*)

But this was insufficient and soon the Cheka and the food detachments were given permission to shoot saboteurs and speculators. Lenin justified the return of capital punishment:

Why does Lenin argue that the law should serve the revolution?

A revolutionary who does not want to be a hypocrite cannot renounce capital punishment. There has never been a revolution or a period of civil war without shootings . . . . In a period of transition laws have only a temporary validity; and when a law hinders the development of the Revolution it must be abolished or amended.
(Quoted in R. Medvedev, *The October Revolution*)

Soon this form of terror was extended to the towns. After a member of the Petrograd Soviet was assassinated by an S.R., Lenin rebuked Zinoviev, head of the Petrograd Soviet:

Comrade Zinoviev, only today we have heard . . . that in Petrograd the workers wanted to reply to the murder of Volodarsky by mass terror and that you . . . restrained them.

I protest most emphatically! . . . The terrorists will consider us old women. This is wartime above all . . . we must encourage the energy and mass character of the terror against the counter-revolutionaries . . . .
(Quoted in R. Medvedev, *The October Revolution*)

By the summer of 1918 the Bolsheviks had made little progress in the villages, and thus the food detachments had little effect. To combat this a

What do these extracts show us about Lenin's attitude and tactics in an emergency?

'Have You Volunteered?' A poster encouraging recruits for the Red Army.

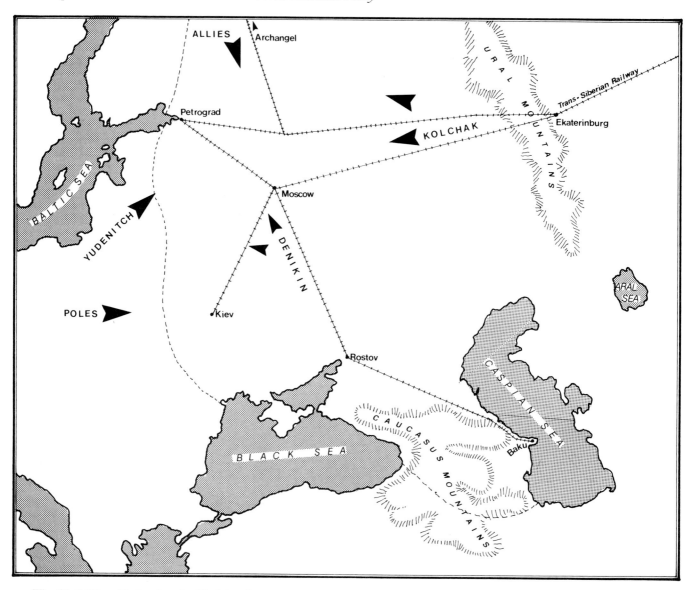

The Civil War. Notice that the 'Reds' retained control of the crucial Moscow-Petrograd axis throughout the conflict.

Alexander Vasiliyevich Kolchak (1870-1920), a vice-admiral before the Revolution, led the White forces afterwards, styling himself 'Supreme Ruler' of Russia.

decree was issued on 11 June 1918, creating Poor Peasant Committees in which the poor of the village were to reorganize themselves to extract grain from the Kulaks. Thus the village was to be divided against itself, the Poor Peasants becoming the Party's representatives in the countryside. Land was taken away from the Kulaks and divided amongst the poor. Lenin later believed this alliance between the poor peasants and the Party to be the turning point in the struggle for power.

This is not the place to describe the course of the Civil War. The opponents of the Bolsheviks (or 'Reds') were called the 'Whites' and their first attacks began early in 1918. Various ex-Tsarist generals, under Admiral Kolchak, led White armies against the Bolsheviks, but while they were aided by the Allies they were not co-ordinated. After the end of the First World War and the subsequent peace with Germany in 1919 the Allies began to withdraw their forces. This was the period of War Communism or Military Communism and one in which the Bolsheviks represented themselves as defenders of both Russia and the Revolution against the Whites and foreign interventionists.

Soviet histories stress the part played by Lenin in organizing Russia during the Civil War. Western writers, on the other hand, stress the key role of Trotsky as leader of the Red Army. To make it more confusing, Trotsky is now virtually a non-person in the Soviet Union and rarely appears in a positive light. Both men played vital roles, each in their very different ways.

Lenin went into every detail of all the major problems connected with the country's defence. From his workroom in the Kremlin he sent out orders, instructions and directives to all parts of the country . . . . Denying himself rest and sleep he followed the progress of military operations and took all steps to ensure victory.
(Anon, *Lenin: A Short Biography*)

The American historian, L. Fischer in his *Life of Lenin*, published in 1965, described Lenin as 'A one man political military staff', and the truth of this is borne out by a selection from Lenin's letters:

Moscow, 29 August 1918

Kedrov was the Bolshevik leader at Vologda in north-eastern Russia.

Comrade Kedrov,
   You send me few facts. Send reports at *every possible opportunity*.
   What fortifications have been built?
   Along which line?
   What points along the railway line have been *safeguarded* by mines . . . .
   Have you safeguarded Vologda sufficiently from the menace of the White Guards? It would be unpardonable if you were to show weakness or negligence in this matter . . . .

Moscow, 25 April 1919

Note to E.M. Sklyansky
   A *fierce* telegram must be sent *today*, signed by you and me, both to the General Headquarters and the C. in C. [Commander in Chief] of Western Front, ordering them to develop the *maximum* of energy and *speed* in the capture of Vilna.

Moscow, 20 October 1919

Comrades [in Tula]!
. . . Look after the defence and watch it closely: are blockhouses being built? Is the work slackening? Have you sufficient material? Workers? Are the Red Army soldiers learning? Are their supplies in order? . . . . You are held wholly responsible for the success of this work or for its failure . . . .

Moscow, 1 February 1920

Find examples in these letters of Lenin's determination, ruthlessness, attention to detail and willingness to take responsibility. Are these essential qualities, and do they support the official 'party line'?

To the Members of the Council of Defence
   The railway transport position is catastrophic. Bread transport to Moscow has ceased. Special measures are essential to save the situation . . . .
1. *Decrease* the individual bread ration for those workers who are not transport workers; *increase* it for transport workers. Let thousands perish, but the country must be saved . . . .
3. Place 30-50 versts, along both sides of the railway, *under martial law*, so as to mobilize workers for the clearing of the track . . . .
(E. Hill and D. Mudie (eds.), *The Letters of Lenin*, 1937)

Not only his letters but his speeches sought to inspire:

The powerful effect of Lenin's speeches is described by A.G. Panyunin, an employee of the Moscow Dynamo Works. 'After hearing his stirring words I felt ready to plunge straight into battle', he wrote. 'Hungry, barefoot, ragged, but filled with enthusiasm and confidence, we drank in every word.'
(Anon, *Lenin: A Short Biography*)

What image of Lenin is portrayed here?

The S.R.s had not forgiven Lenin for signing a treaty with Germany.

On 30 August 1918 Lenin was shot by an S.R., Dora Kaplan. He was badly wounded and came near to death. In September 1918 *Pravda* wrote:

Armed volunteers, including a large number of women, ready to fight against the White leader General Denekin.

The Czechs had been captured by the Russians while fighting in the Austro-Hungarian Army. Their main aim was to return to their new country, Czechoslovakia. Eventually they left Russia via the Trans-Siberian Railway and Vladivostok.

Lenin is conquering his illness. He will conquer it! For so wills the proletariat. Such is its command to Destiny!

By 8 September Lenin was well enough to send the following telegram to the 5th Army Headquarters in Sviyazhsk in answer to wishes for his speedy recovery:

Thanks. Excellent progress towards recovery. Convinced that quelling the Kazan Czechs and White Guards and their bloodthirsty Kulak supporters will be a model of mercilessness.
(E. Hill and D. Mudie (eds.) *The Letters of Lenin*)

The N.E.P.
By the end of 1921 the Civil War was over, but the country was devastated. Famine and drought were widespread and Russia's grain production was less than half that of 1913, while her pig iron production was only 3 per cent of its former level. Discontent was rife in the countryside, and in the towns industry was at a virtual standstill. To add to the problems of the Communists, early 1921 saw strikes in Petrograd, whilst the sailors at the nearby naval base at Kronstadt called for basic freedoms, elections, and a lessening of control by the ruling party.

*Lenin speaking in Red Square on the first
anniversary of the Revolution, 7 November
1918.*

Lenin's funeral in Red Square, January 1924.

In March 1921 the Tenth Bolshevik Party Congress opened in Petrograd. Lenin seized the opportunity to introduce a New Economic Policy (the N.E.P.). Agricultural production had to be increased and the peasants won over; industry had to be regenerated, trade boosted and foreign capital secured to aid the recovery. Lenin admitted to Party delegates that mistakes had been made, that the pace of change had been too fast. He introduced a tax on grain, allowed private trading, so that peasants could sell their surpluses at market.

Lenin freely admitted that the N.E.P. was a retreat, but stressed that it was necessary:

> We have sinned . . . in going too far in nationalizing trade and industry, in closing down local commerce. Was this a mistake? Undoubtedly.
> (Quoted in A. Ulam, *Lenin and the Bolsheviks*)

The New Economic Policy (1921-8) was the replacement for War Communism.

Lenin realized that whilst concessions were necessary in industry and agriculture, it was essential to tighten the control of the Party. The Kronstadt Revolt was put down ruthlessly by Trotsky, while the Tenth Party Congress initiated the process by which the Communist Party became the only legal party, and membership of it was regularly vetted to ensure that only true Communists were Party members. Stalin became the General Secretary in control of Party records. At first this post was regarded as routine, deserving of a dull but loyal member like Stalin. He

Trotsky led the Red Army across the ice to the naval base of Kronstadt, which is about 14 miles west of Leningrad in the Gulf of Finland. Why was it essential to crush the revolt before the ice melted?

had acquitted himself well in 1917, and acted with firmness and ruthlessness as Commissar for Nationalities in bringing back into the fold the republics which had declared their independence.

Increasingly, from 1921 until his death in January 1924, Lenin fought against declining health. The assassination attempt was followed by several strokes, which were made worse by overwork. In March 1923 he suffered his third major stroke and lost the power of speech. He was still determined to continue but in his last months he was increasingly rationed in his reading, and command was removed from his hands.

In his last years Lenin became increasingly concerned for Russia after his death, and worried about who should succeed him. On 25 December 1922 he dictated a testament stating his views on the succession after his death. He feared a split in the Party; he saw Trotsky as too individual and self-confident, but it was Stalin who worried him most:

Since Comrade Stalin has become General Secretary, he holds immense power in his hands, and I am not convinced that he will always know how to use this power with the necessary moderation.
(Quoted in G. von Rauch, *A History of Soviet Russia*)

On 4 January 1923 Lenin added a further comment:

Stalin is too rude and this failing . . . is intolerable in the office of General Secretary. Therefore I propose to the Comrades to find a way to remove Stalin from this post . . . .
(Quoted in G. von Rauch, *A History of Soviet Russia*)

After Lenin's death in January 1924 the testament was not made public and was suppressed out of loyalty to the Party. Stalin organized a magnificent funeral, while Trotsky was convalescing in the south, and within five years was in complete control of the Party and of Russia.

Conclusions

Seven days after Lenin's death, on 28 January 1924, Stalin delivered a lecture to the Kremlin Military Students. In it he talked of his first meeting with Lenin in 1903, and then went on to recall his qualities. The printed article has headings such as 'Modesty', 'Strength of Logic', 'No Boasting', 'Man of Principle', 'Confidence in the Masses' and 'Genius of Revolution'. He concluded:

Brilliant foresight, the ability rapidly to catch and appreciate the inner sense of impending events – this is the feature of Lenin – that enabled him to outline the correct strategy and a clear line of conduct at the turning points of the revolutionary movement.
(J. Stalin, *Lenin*)

Can you identify particular 'turning points' where Lenin acted decisively?

Robin Bruce Lockhart, a British Consular Official in Moscow, first met Lenin in the spring of 1918. He wrote:

Lenin speaks to H.G. Wells in his Kremlin office, 6 October 1920.

There was nothing in his personal appearance to suggest even faintly a resemblance to the super-man. Short of stature, rather plump, with short, thick

neck, broad shoulders, round, red face, high intellectual forehead, nose slightly turned up, brownish moustache, and short stubby beard, he looked at the first glance more like a provincial grocer than a leader of men. Yet in those steely eyes there was something that arrested my attention, something in that quizzing, half-contemptuous, half-smiling look which spoke of boundless self confidence and conscious superiority . . . . I was . . . impressed by his tremendous will power, his relentless determination and his lack of emotion.
(R.H. Bruce Lockhart, *Memoirs of a British Agent*, 1932)

In 1921 Armand Hammer, a young American businessman, had an hour-long meeting with the Soviet leader:

. . . I walked to Lenin's office on the second floor of a large building in . . . the Kremlin . . . . The room was very small and unpretentious, full of books, magazines and newspapers in half a dozen languages. They were everywhere . . . save for a clear space occupied by a battery of telephones.
   During . . . our conversation . . . I was completely absorbed by Lenin's personality. His powers of concentration were tremendous. When he talked to you, he made you feel you were the most important person in his life.
(A. Hammer, *Hammer: Witness to History*, 1987)

In September 1920 H.G. Wells, the famous English author, visited Russia and met Lenin in the Kremlin. He was surprised:

After the tiresome class-war fanatics I had been encountering among the Communists, men of formulae as sterile as flints, after numerous experiences of the trained and empty conceit of the common Marxist devotee, this amazing little man, with his frank admission of the immensity and complication of the project of Communism . . . was very refreshing.
(H.G. Wells, *Russia in the Shadows*, 1921)

Wells had noted a characteristic which is essential to an understanding of Lenin; that of flexibility and adaptability. He knew when to change and adapt. He recognized this himself and worked hard at it.
   In 1920 Lenin told a group of foreign sympathizers:

The whole history of Bolshevism, before and after the October Revolution, is full of instances of manoeuvring, agreements and compromises with others.
(Quoted in J. Keep, 'Lenin as Tactician', in L. Schapiro and P. Reddaway (eds.), *Lenin: A Reappraisal*, 1967)

An American biographer of Lenin has written:

As a statesman, Lenin observed, weighed, and reasoned, and arrived at decisions on the basis of reality. Power did not go to his head. It cleared it . . . . [For] Lenin, power was too precious to be squandered on consistency. His responsibilities compelled a cold, objective assessment of circumstances, compelled a sober, practical unsentimentality stripped of illusions, slogans, cant, pride, attachment to theory, and attachment to past stands and statements.
(L. Fischer, *Lenin*, 1965)

So how can we conclude? Leonard Schapiro, a British historian who was born in Russia and as a child lived through the events of 1917, has written that:

From the age of seventeen . . . [Lenin's] life had been devoted to the aim of revolution. He played no part in February [March] 1917 when the monarchy collapsed: His sights were set on the only kind of revolution that he acknowledged,

---

Armand Hammer arranged trading agreements with Soviet Russia in the 1920s. He is now a multimillionaire, and still visits Russia.

Make a list of the personal characteristics of Lenin that made him a great revolutionary leader. (Use the eye witness accounts of Bruce Lockhart, Hammer and Wells.)

Тов. Ленин ОЧИЩАЕТ землю от нечисти.

A Bolshevik poster. Which groups is Lenin sweeping away?

one in which the Bolshevik party, created by him in 1903, would hold the monopoly of power in the name of the working class. Other socialist parties . . . were to be excluded as fraudulent pretenders. All methods were justified to achieve this end, because Lenin and his close supporters believed with fanatical intensity that their success in Petrograd on 25 October 1917 would inaugurate a new era in the history of mankind, and would bring forth a new and happier world. This faith may have diminished as the practical problems of office accumulated . . . . But to ignore the faith that dominated Lenin . . . is to misunderstand the history of the Russian Revolution . . . there is no doubt that without Lenin the Bolshevik coup would have been postponed, and might conceivably have failed.
(L. Schapiro, *1917*)

Having gained power Lenin steered the Bolsheviks through the next four difficult years, prepared to be ruthless and use force when necessary.

A large hoarding erected for May Day in Leningrad.

Armand Hammer defends Lenin:

Lenin has been called ruthless and fanatical, cruel and cold. I refuse to believe it. It was his intense human sympathy, his personal magnetism and lack of self interest, that made him great . . . .

Does this argument ring true?
(A. Hammer, *Hammer: Witness to History*)

Nevertheless, Lenin's ruthlessness in part explains why his critics have seen him and his works as the forerunners of Stalin and Stalinism.

Was Stalin Lenin's heir? Was his horrendous period of rule a direct consequence of the régime instituted by Lenin? These questions have much preoccupied historians and there is no agreement on the answers. The matter is complicated by the fact that those who seek to preserve the idea of Communism from

contamination by Stalin's misdeeds, which few now defend, try to place the greatest possible distance between Lenin and his successor. . . . Stalinism was not a necessary consequence of the mission, but it was nevertheless a possible result. There was nothing inevitable about the emergence of a man of Stalin's character; yet once it happened, the tools were ready to his hand.
(L. Schapiro, *1917*)

Would you say this was a balanced judgment?

For Roy Medvedev, a Soviet historian whose books have been published in the West (though not in his own country), Lenin is the hero-figure before everything in Russia went wrong under Stalin:

Do you think saving the Bolshevik regime was worth a civil war and millions of deaths?

. . . . Can there really be any comparison between decisions taken at the height of the Civil War and decisions arrived at in peacetime? Can the Red terror of 1918-20 really be equated with the terror inflicted on the country by Stalin in 1929-32 or 1936-8? In the first case it was a question of saving the Soviet state from certain downfall; later it was the consolidation of Stalin's one-man dictatorship . . . .

What is the distinction Medvedev makes between Lenin and Stalin?

Undoubtedly Lenin was a man fanatically dedicated to the idea of power, but it was the power of the proletariat, the power of the Communist Party . . . it was never a question of personal power . . . . Stalin, on the other hand, was fanatically dedicated to the quest for personal power . . . . In essence, Lenin and Stalin have almost nothing in common as human beings or as political personalities.
(R. Medvedev, *On Stalin and Stalinism*, 1979)

A view of the Moscow River from the Kremlin.

Workers' flats in present-day Leningrad.

Whatever one's personal judgment on Lenin it is unquestionable that he is one of history's 'great men'.

Communists (who usually play down the role of the individual in history) and non-Communists alike are agreed on the unique contribution of Lenin's genius. 'The role of personality,' wrote Trotsky, 'arises here before us on a truly gigantic scale.' Lenin brought revolution to a country where, traditionally, Marxists had least expected it.

Would Lenin have appreciated the Soviet Union of today? The Bolsheviks had set out to create the freest society in the world. In his blueprint for Soviet society, composed on the eve of the Bolshevik Revolution, Lenin confidently wrote:

> We ourselves, the workers, will organize large-scale production on the basis of what capitalism has already created . . . we will reduce the role of the state officials to that of simply carrying out our instructions as . . . modestly paid 'foremen and accountants'. Such a beginning . . . will of itself lead to the gradual 'withering away' of all bureaucracy . . .
> (Quoted in D. McLellan, *Karl Marx: The Legacy*, 1983)

This picture accords little with the reality of Soviet society today. Indeed one is led to doubt just how revolutionary the Revolution has been. Lenin and his followers believed that revolution in Russia would lead to revolution in the industrialized West. This has not happened. Inside the Soviet Union, by the 1930s, a new autocrat and the familiar centralized bureaucracy had emerged. The wheel had come full circle. The Soviet Union today has the superpower status that the tsars craved, but can still be scathingly described by critics as an 'Upper Volta with rockets'. A British newspaper correspondent can write that:

Many of these criticisms and weaknesses are being tackled by Gorbachev. Find examples of these from the national press. Why does he argue that he is trying to return to Leninism?

The most powerful impression that strikes the newcomer to the USSR is its Third-Worldishness: the tacky and dilapidated surroundings, the decay even of recent buildings, the drabness; above all the people's idle apathy and drink-sodden fatalism in the face of decades of coercion, negligence, hypocrisy and tyranny. Russia is not a modern country.
(Xan Smiley, 'The Dowdy Face of Third World Russia', *Sunday Telegraph*, 1987)

Much that exists in the USSR today – the economic backwardness and sluggishness, the corruption, the privileged lives of the Communist Party élite – makes a mockery of all that Lenin struggled for. Yet Lenin is still the centre of an extraordinary cult – he is as important dead as he ever was alive. Perhaps this is what would horrify Lenin most of all if he were to rise from his Red Square Mausoleum.

Whether the present Party Secretary, Mikhail Gorbachev, will be able to achieve all the much needed reforms remains to be seen. Certainly, at the time of writing he appears to have made an impressive start. His policies of openness (*glasnost*) and reconstruction (*perestroika*) are advocated as a return to the principles of Lenin, and have been welcomed throughout the world.

Lenin's Contemporaries

Alexander II (1818-81). Ruled Russia from 1855 until his assassination in 1881 by the People's Will. Emancipated the serfs in 1861 and was responsible for a number of important reforms in the 1860s. He was determined to maintain Russia's position as a great power in Europe.

Brusilov, Alexei A. (1853-1925). Russian general in the First World War, responsible for the last major offensive against the Germans. He later joined the Red Army.

Gorky, Maxim (1868-1936). Leading Russian playwright, author and editor. Self educated, his autobiographies *My Childhood* (1913), *My Apprenticeship* (1918) and *My Universities* (1923) are very moving accounts of his earlier life. Although in favour of the Bolsheviks, he opposed their seizure of power. Lived in Italy from 1921 to 1928, then returned to Russia and became a close friend of Stalin.

Kamenev, Lev B. (1833-1936). A leading Bolshevik, he opposed the seizure of power in 1917, but remained a prominent Party member. Later involved in struggles with Stalin, he was imprisoned and then executed in 1936.

Kerensky, Alexander F. (1881-1970). Moderate Socialist Revolutionary member of the Duma. Minister of Justice and later Prime Minister of the Provisional Government and member of the Soviet. He was abroad in November 1917, and from 1946 lived in the USA.

Kornilov, General (1870-1918). Commander in Chief of the Armed Forces in August 1917. Staged a coup against Kerensky, and later joined the Whites in the Civil War and was killed in action.

Krupskaya, Nadezhda K. (1869-1939). A teacher, she married Lenin in 1898 and went with him into exile. After the Revolution she became Vice Commissar for Education and a member of the Central Committee.

Lvov, Prince Georgy Y. (1861-1925). Active in the Zemstvo Movement, he was Prime Minister of the First Provisional Government. He later lived in exile in France.

Martov, Yuly O. (1873-1923). Leader of the Mensheviks, he parted company with Lenin in 1903. He was later exiled and lived in Berlin.

Marx, Karl H. (1818-83). German writer and philosopher. He left Germany after the failure of the revolution in 1848. Settled in London where he worked in the British Museum and wrote *Das Kapital* (1867). Buried in Highgate Cemetery, London.

Nicholas II (1868-1918). The last tsar of Russia. Ruled from 1894 until his abdication in 1917. Much influenced by his wife, he was also crucially absent from the centre of power when he took charge at the Front in 1915. Executed by the Bolsheviks at Ekaterinburg in 1918.

Plekhanov, Georgy V. (1857-1918). Founded the Liberation of Labour Group in 1883. Worked with Lenin, but in 1903 joined the Mensheviks. Regarded as the founder of Russian Marxism.

Rasputin, Gregory Y. (1872-1916). Siberian peasant and later 'holy man'. Influenced the tsarina because he was able to help her son Alexis who had a rare blood disease, haemophilia, which Rasputin treated by hypnotism. Gained undue influence when the tsar went to the Front. He was assassinated in December 1916 by Prince Yusopov, who hoped to save the monarchy by disposing of him.

Solzhenitsyn, Alexander I. (1918-   ). Writer and dissident, now in exile in the USA. Spent eight years in the labour camps under Stalin. On his release he wrote *One Day in the Life of Ivan Denisovich* (1962) which was published in Russia. It described life in the camps. He was arrested and deported in 1974.

Stalin, Joseph V. (1879-1953). Born in Georgia. Joined the R.S.D.L.P. and later the Bolsheviks. Active revolutionary and editor of *Pravda*. Commissar for Nationalities after the Revolution, he became General Secretary of the Communist Party in 1922. Emerged from the struggle for power as the supreme leader, eliminating his rivals and ruling through a reign of terror.

Stolypin, Peter A. (1862-1911). Minister of the Interior from 1906, when he introduced various agricultural reforms. Assassinated by a Socialist Revolutionary in 1911.

Trotsky, Lev D. (1879-1940). Joined the R.S.D.L.P. in 1896, but in 1903 became a Menshevik. Following his part in the 1905 revolution he went into exile, returning to Russia in February 1917. He had a major role in both the Bolshevik seizure of power and the Civil War. Expelled from the Party in 1927 and from the Soviet Union in 1929. Murdered by one of Stalin's agents in 1940 in Mexico.

Book List

Anon, *Lenin for Beginners*, Writers & Readers, 1977.

Anon, *V.I. Lenin: A Short Biography*, Progress Publishers, Moscow, 1979.

Brogan, H, *The Life of Arthur Ransome*, Jonathan Cape, 1984.

Bunyan, J. and Fisher, H.H. (eds), *The Bolshevik Revolution, 1917-1918*, Stanford University Press, 1934.

Browder, R.P. and Kerensky, A.F. (eds.), *The Russian Provisional Government, 1917*, Stanford University Press, 1961.

Campling, E., *Living Through History: The Russian Revolution*, Batsford, 1985.

Carr, H., *The Russian Revolution from Lenin to Stalin, 1917-29*, Macmillan, 1979.

Carrère D'Encausse, H., *Lenin: Revolution and Power*, Longman, 1982.

Catchpole, B., *A Map History of Russia*, Heinemann, 1974.

Conquest, R., *Lenin*, Fontana, 1972.

Curtiss, J.S., *The Russian Revolutions of 1917*, Von Nostrand, 1957.

Fitzpatrick, S., *The Russian Revolution 1917-1932*, Oxford, 1982.

Hill, C., *Lenin and the Russian Revolution*, Penguin, 1971.

Hill, E. and Mudie, D. (eds.), *The Letters of Lenin*, Chapman and Hall, c.1935.

Krupskaya, N.K., *Memories of Lenin*, New York International Publishers, 1930.

Lenin, V.I., *What is to be Done?*, Martin Lawrence, c. 1935

Lockhart, R.H. Bruce, *Memoirs of a British Agent* (1932), Macmillan, 1985.

Mack, D., *Lenin and the Russian Revolution*, Longman, 1984.

Maxton, J., *Lenin*, Peter Davies, 1932.

McLellan, D., *Karl Marx: The Legacy*, BBC, 1983.

Medvedev, R., *The October Revolution*, Constable, 1979.

Medvedev, R., *On Stalin and Stalinism*, Oxford University Press, 1979.

Nevinson, H.W., *The Dawn in Russia*, Harper, 1906.

Paxton, J., *Companion to Russian History*, Batsford, 1983.

Rauch, G. von, *A History of Soviet Russia*, (1967), Praeger, sixth edition, 1972.

Reed, J., *Ten Days that Shook the World*, (1926), Penguin, 1974.

Robottom, J., *Russia in Change 1870-1945*, Longman, 1987.

Schapiro, L. and Reddaway, P. (eds.), *Lenin: A Reappraisal*, Pall Mall, 1967.

Service, R., *The Russian Revolution 1900-1927*, Macmillan, 1986.

Shub, D., *Lenin: A Biography*, (1948), Penguin, 1966.

Solzhenitsyn, A., *Lenin in Zurich*, Bodley Head, 1976.

Stalin, J., *Lenin*, International Publishers, 1934.

Tarnovsky, K., *Illustrated History of the U.S.S.R.*, Novosti Press, 1982.

Trotsky, L., *The History of the Russian Revolution*, first published 1932-3, Gollancz, 1965.

Tumarkin, N., *Lenin Lives!*, Harvard, 1983.

Ulam, A.B., *Lenin and the Bolsheviks*, Fontana/Collins, 1965.

Valentinov, N. (Volsky), *Encounters with Lenin*, Oxford University Press, 1968.

Wells, H.G., *Russia in the Shadows*, Hodder and Stoughton, 1921.

Wolfe, B.D., *Three Men who Made a Revolution*, (1948), Penguin, 1984.

Index